WRITING FOR THE WEB:
GEEKS' EDITION

WRITING FOR THE WEB: GEEKS' EDITION

Crawford Kilian

Self-Counsel Press
(a division of)
International Self-Counsel Press Ltd.
USA   Canada

Self-Counsel Press acknowledges the financial support of the Government of Canada through the Book Publishing Industry Development Program (BPIDP) for our publishing activities.

Printed in Canada

First edition: 2000

Canadian Cataloguing in Publication Data
Kilian, Crawford, 1941–
　　Writing for the web: geeks' edition

　　(Self-counsel computer series)
　　ISBN 1-55180-303-8

　　1. World Wide Web 2. English language — Rhetoric — Data processing. 3. Web sites — Design.
I. Title II. Series.

TK5105.888.K542 2000　　　　808'.066005　　　　C00-910876-9

Self-Counsel Press
(a division of)
International Self-Counsel Press Ltd.

1704 North State Street　　　　1481 Charlotte Road
Bellingham, WA 98225　　　　North Vancouver, BC V7J 1H1
USA　　　　　　　　　　　　　Canada

This book is dedicated to all those friends and colleagues
who participated in the creation of this book,
and to everyone who helps to create the Web by writing for it.

CONTENTS

PREFACE

For more than 30 years, I've taught workplace writing, freelance article writing, and how to write commercial fiction. My newspaper and magazine articles number well over 600. This is my 20th book. So I'm pretty dedicated to print on paper as a medium of communication.

But in the late 1980s, I began to see how networked computers were changing the way we communicate. In some ways they were just another means of getting print on paper, but something about the medium was changing the nature of our messages. First in email, and then on the World Wide Web, we were writing, reading, and reacting to information in different ways.

In teaching technology students in the early 1990s, I had to learn fast to stay ahead of them. We were all scrambling to master the new grammar of multimedia: the ways that text and sound and images could combine to express ideas. With few authorities to turn to, the best way to learn seemed to be to watch what we ourselves were doing and try to draw general principles from our experience.

By the mid-1990s, the Web was becoming truly worldwide, and a whole new industry arose to serve and advance it. I got a sense of how big it was when I walked into a university bookstore and found, by rough estimate, 170 shelf-feet of books on the Web: how to master HTML, CGI, and Java; how to use this or that browser; how to design Websites; how to research the exponentially growing resources available on the Web.

Not one of those books dealt with the actual words to be used on the Web.

Well, that made a certain amount of sense. No one had enough experience yet to say just what would work on the Web and what wouldn't. Hypertext had been around in various forms since the 1970s, but it wouldn't necessarily work on the Web the way it does in, for example, a CD-ROM encyclopedia. So most of the Web pioneers wrote in whatever style seemed comfortable, and other pioneers followed their lead; that's why so many writers say things like "Check it out" and "This site under construction."

A few people began to question some of the writing on the Web, and their own Websites offered guidance. Even Tim Berners-Lee, the father of the World Wide Web, put up a style guide. But such sites were scarce, lost in the explosive growth of the Web during the late 1990s.

Meanwhile, creating Websites had changed from a self-taught skill into an industry. The pioneers had given countless hours to trial and error, mostly error, in learning the basics of a new technology. But they couldn't squander their time when clients were paying for it. An obscure computer specialty in 1992 had become almost a basic job skill by the end of the decade. My own colleagues, teaching in fields like tourism and business administration, began to wonder how they could cram Web design courses into an already crowded curriculum. If they couldn't, their graduates risked losing out to Web-skilled competitors.

So the time seemed right for a book that might help both Web experts and newcomers save time and avoid known pitfalls. It might thereby help Web users as well.

No doubt this book reflects my own biases toward print on paper, but I have tried to learn from a wide range of self-taught pioneer Web authorities and to present their views as well as my own. If my arguments make sense and help you write successful Webtext, of course I'll be delighted. But I look forward also to being rebutted and superseded, because better insights will make the Web a more effective communication tool for all of us. Some of my arguments may provoke you into articulating contrary views that work to make your sites succeed; if so, this book has succeeded too.

In mastering writing for the Web, we learn about what goes on in other kinds of writing as well, and what goes on in our own minds. So in learning how to write well for this medium, I think we can learn how to write better in all media, and we can learn something about ourselves as well.

ACKNOWLEDGMENTS

As I look back on the creation of this book, I can see it's been a highly interactive process. Many people responded to early versions or excerpts from it, making me reconsider my early views.

I thank the online colleagues who graciously permitted me to quote from their email correspondence, Websites, and published books: Tara Calishain, Nancy Eaton, Robert E. Horn, Alex and Irene Kirkwood, Stephen Martin, Jakob Nielsen, Gareth Rees, John S. Rhodes, Marijke Rijsberman, Lisa Schmitt, and Karen Solomon. Thanks also to the many others who volunteered their Websites as possible case studies; if I'd had the space I'd have gladly included them all. A special thank-you to Steve Outing and Amy Gahran, owners of the Online Writers listserv which has helped us all to understand this medium better.

My own students have contributed greatly to my understanding of online writing, and I should thank those in particular who prodded me to make myself clearer as I taught (and learned) the principles of hypertext writing: Bev Chiu, David Ingram, Raj Kamal, Sarah King, Adrian McInnes, Ross McKerlich, Sandy Meyer, Michelle Morelos, Gabriela Schonbach, Michael Souvage, and Lucy Wang.

I also thank Judy Phillips, who edited the first edition of *Writing for the Web*, and Richard Day, who edited this *Geeks' Edition*.

INTRODUCTION

The glory and the curse of the World Wide Web in its first decade is that no one truly understands it.

Its glory is that the Web involves a whole new medium of communication that will inspire us, eventually, to think and express ourselves in new ways. But, just as our ancestors saw the automobile as only a conveniently horseless carriage, the curse of the Web is that we are bringing our previous experience and habits to it, which colors how we create and use it.

So television stations treat the Web like very slow television. Newspapers treat it like a newspaper pasted onto the side of a packing crate. Businesses treat the Web like the Yellow Pages, only with more colors. And most Website creators treat it like whatever medium they're already familiar with: a sheet of typing paper, a canvas, a comic strip, a family photo album, a library, or a Rolodex.

While the Web can indeed serve all those functions, one of its primary purposes is to make large amounts of text accessible online. (The Latin word for "web," by the way, is *textus.*) Bells and whistles (in the form of graphics and sound) can make a Website resemble a medieval illuminated manuscript, but on most sites they're still essentially decorative rather than functional items — just as the elaborate designs on medieval manuscripts functioned simply to make the texts prettier. Since many Web users have spent more time watching television than reading, the graphic elements of a Website are especially important to them, but text remains the core of most Websites.

Surprisingly, the hundreds of Web-related books recently published have ignored this fact. These books explain many different ways to tweak hypertext markup language (HTML), but offer very little advice on what words to put inside the HTML.

This book offers just such advice.

The Web is a very different medium from print and television, but our print and television habits influence the way we respond to text on the computer monitor. (We even call Web files "pages" when they're really nothing of the sort.) We read print documents in a certain way, using subtle cues to navigate through a familiar format: the indented first line of a paragraph tells us a new topic is coming up; page numbers establish a sequence; indexes use alphabetical order. But the print format doesn't apply on the Web. We surf through television channels with our remote control, and we bring the same attitude to the television-like monitor of our computers: Deliver something interesting right now, some kind of jolt or reward, or we'll go somewhere else.

These responses to the Web demand a kind of writing that is different from other media — not better or worse, just different. Effective Website creation doesn't mean only cool video, graphics, and sound; it also means text that will halt impatient surfers and make them read what you've written.

This book offers some principles for composing text for your Website. The principles aren't carved in stone, but they arise from the experience of thousands of people writing online and on the Web over the past decade and more — experience reported by analysts like Jakob Nielsen, an engineer who's been studying computer-mediated communications since the early 1980s. We can draw some general conclusions about what works and what doesn't; we can also ignore or modify those conclusions if our own circumstances require it. When George Orwell compiled his list of rules for clear writing, he saved the best for last: "Break any of these rules sooner than say something outright barbarous."

Good Webtext has a lot in common with good print text. It's plain, concise, concrete, and "transparent": Even on a personal site, the text shouldn't draw attention to itself, only to its subject. This book will give you plenty of exercises and tips for developing such a writing style.

Like good print text, Webtext carries a nonverbal message or subtext. The message may be, "I'm comfortable with this medium and I understand you, my reader." Or it may be, "I'm completely wrapped up in my own ego and my love of cool stuff." This book should help sensitize you to any writing habits that may unconsciously let the wrong subtext slip out.

This book won't tell you how to design your site, or how to insert animated images — what Web designers call "dancing baloney" — into your Web pages. But it will try to alert you to the likely consequences of your design decisions. If you like long, long paragraphs full of long, long words, for example, your readers will quickly lose interest in what you have to say. Similarly, if your Web page scrolls on forever, you will also lose readers. If you build your site with layer after layer of linked pages, you will likely baffle, if not bore, your readers. And if you use some knockout graphic you have fallen in love with, it may completely distract attention from your text.

If you are creating your own personal or commercial site, you decide both the content and the structure of the site: what its topics are, how big it is, how its pages connect, how its graphics and text (and maybe audio and video) work together. You will rapidly learn that you can undercut yourself by presenting text as if it were still on paper, for reasons we'll discuss in this book. So it's in your own interest to understand something about Website design basics, especially as they affect the display of text.

If you are writing text for a site designed by someone else, you face other constraints. The site designers may not have known (or cared) about the kind of text displays you think you need. Navigation aids may not be good enough, or the design may dictate that text be chopped up in confusing ways. All too often, the people who decide the structural issues of a Website are themselves not very experienced with using the Web. If they're the Home Page Committee of your organization, they may be concerned only about the organization having a presence on the Web or with the image the organization presents to the world, but not about the usefulness of the site. Chapter 6 discusses writing for corporate sites in more detail.

How you deal with the political problems of getting good text onto your Website is only one of your challenges as a Webwriter. You may need to explain some basics about the medium to your colleagues, and, again, while this book doesn't deal directly with design issues, you do need to understand some realities about the medium if you're going to use it effectively. And whether you're writing for a personal or a corporate Website, effectiveness is the whole point of your effort.

This book is not intended to give details of how to write and market online journalism, or how to develop online course content, though the prominence of such genres on the Web is increasing. But the general issues discussed in the book should give you some useful pointers for specific kinds of Webwriting.

▶   ▶   ▶

So let's start at the beginning, with what makes your computer monitor a different medium from this printed page.

Computers condition us for "high joltage." A "jolt" is an emotional reward that follows a prescribed action. Turn on the television at the right time for your favorite program and it delivers jolts. Watch a movie and it delivers jolts, and so does a well-written book. Log on to your favorite newsgroup and every new insult you send to the idiot you're flaming delivers jolts.

Like Pavlov's dogs, computer users are now conditioned to expect such stimuli. Maybe it's a jolt of surprise as our computer beeps or boings. Maybe it's a jolt of interest as we find information we've been hunting for, or a jolt of pleasure as someone praises our last brilliant post to a newsgroup. (Just discovering the Web itself, with its promise of endless jolts, is a powerful jolt.) But we feel deprived if we don't get some kind of jolt at regular intervals, so we go where we hope to find more stimulation which, on the Web, means Websites.

Does this mean your site has to look and sound like a rock video? Or that you need to use obscene language in order to get and keep readers' attention? Not at all. A truly high-joltage Website is one that supplies the information its readers are looking for, and it certainly doesn't have to be expressed in an outlandish or tasteless manner. But your text had better look invitingly brief, and it should provide at least the simple jolt of being understandable in one quick glance. If it also intrigues readers by offering a hook of some kind so they'll keep reading, so much the better. Your role as a Web author is to make your reader's job effortless.

▶   ▶   ▶

To sum up: By combining text, graphics, and sound, the World Wide Web gives the Internet some of the qualities of familiar media, such as print, television, movies, and radio. When we recognize those familiar qualities, we respond to the Internet as if we were dealing with print or television or radio. As a Webwriter, you should recognize this mindset and write your text accordingly.

But Webwriters also have to accept the strengths and weaknesses of the Web. While your readers may want to treat your Website like a book or magazine or television show, it's still a Website — a collection of electronic files which you may organize as you see fit, but which your readers will read in any sequence they like. That puts you in an interesting bind because, while your readers will read your site as text, and you may think of it as text, it's really hypertext. In Chapter 1, we'll look at what that means for you as a Webwriter.

Note: All efforts have been made to verify the accuracy of URLs in this book upon publication. However, since Website addresses are constantly changing, not every cited URL may be accessible. If you find a particular URL does not lead to the indicated site, a search engine may help find the site's new or alternative location.

Introduction to Geeks' Edition

Since the first edition of this book came out in the spring of 1999, reader response has been very encouraging. But things happen fast in the world of the Web, and it soon became clear that the book needed to provide more than I had expected, and for a wider readership.

The "early adopters" of this book have been largely people who develop Web content either full-time or as part of some nontechnical but Web-related work. They've got good writing skills and often some technical skills as well, but they needed more examples of Webtext (especially editing). Many are also early adopters of the Web as a career, and are looking for insights into the demands of a growing market — how to find freelance opportunities, how to land a full-time Webwriting job, how to put Webwriting into the curriculum.

As well, it seemed clear that the book neglected another important readership: the technically skilled people who design Websites, but who also have the job of writing content. With relatively little writing experience, these people face a real challenge — especially if their bosses think that "content development" means uploading news releases and annual reports, and nothing more.

A third readership also needed attention. These are the content developers who write in English learned as a second or third language. They do dramatic and exciting work in this medium, but the English language is full of pitfalls for them. Even simple business abbreviations can be unbreakable code for such writers, yet their success hinges on understanding not only standard English but countless dialects as well: technical English, business English, Australian or Canadian or South African English.

All these readers are, in the current use of the term, "geeks" — people who not only do their job, but love their job. What's more, as geeks they go on learning their job; it always offers more surprises and challenges, which is one reason why they love it.

So this edition is an attempt to show you writing geeks, and technical geeks, and international geeks, more of the surprises and challenges of writing for the Web. You can use this book as a self-teaching manual, as a classroom textbook, and as a useful reference tool you can store in your own "geekosphere" (the environment immediately around your computer). And while it's print on paper — treeware, in geekspeak — this book tries to be as interactive as possible. It offers dozens of links to relevant Websites (and those links are as updated and accurate as I could make them). It also offers links to me, so that you can tell me directly about the errors you've found in it, or your disagreements with my arguments. I'll be delighted to respond, and to learn all I can from your experience. I'd better — this probably won't be the last edition of *Writing for the Web*, and the Web will keep changing. May you and I keep changing too.

1
HYPE AND HYPERTEXT

When early computer users and researchers began to see how they could navigate through electronic information and link one item to another using something called hypertext, they realized that it would offer readers an amazing power and freedom.

If you want to learn about, say, vampires, you face a pretty tedious process if you plan to research the topic using a multi-volume encyclopedia. First you would go to the volume with all the V entries, and find "Vampires." That entry may suggest you also look at entries in other volumes: Transylvania; Dracula; Stoker, Bram; Lugosi, Bela; films, horror; bats, vampire; films, German: Nosferatu… As you consult each of these entries, you're pulling heavy volumes off the shelf and replacing them, making notes, and generally taking up a lot of time.

Even using a single-volume book to research a topic presents challenges. Such a book may have its own hypertext in the form of footnotes, end notes, appendixes, bibliographies, and an index — even marginal scribbles by the last reader. The researcher looking for particular information soon learns to read backward: start with the index and then jump to just the pages dealing with the subject of interest. Even then, the follow-up of tracking down footnoted references and finding titles mentioned in the bibliography can be tedious and frustrating.

Hypertext saves you much of that work. Each hypertext document has electronic links to other hypertext documents, much like doors between

What Is Hypertext, Anyway?
An essay or paper with footnotes or a bibliography is a kind of hypertext since it refers to other documents in a way that makes it fairly easy to find them. A document with marginal annotations or some other kind of commentary can also be called hypertext. But in this book, "hypertext" refers to a document in electronic format (i.e., a file on a computer hard drive or a CD-ROM containing text, graphics, audio, video, or some combination of these elements), linked to other such electronic documents. The link enables readers to jump between documents — even if the documents are on remote computers far away from one another.

rooms in a library. If you're reading a hypertext document about horror films and you find a mention of Bela Lugosi, the actor's name can itself be a link to still more information. Instead of making notes, you can simply save the file about Lugosi along with all the other items you've encountered.

And if you don't want to read about Bela Lugosi, but you do want to read about vampire bats or Transylvanian history, you can ignore the link to the Hollywood star and continue your reading.

This freedom of choice has its attractions, but some hypertext pioneers have tried to make it look like a revolution on a Gutenbergian scale. They claim that, freed from the tyranny of the author's structure, readers can now examine any document they like, in any order they choose, and use the information any way they please. (Of course, readers can also read a print document any way they please, but it takes more effort to jump back and forth in a print-on-paper document than in an electronic document.) If each item of information is small enough, maybe just a paragraph or even a sentence, then readers have even more freedom. Instead of being led like children by the author's hand, readers can now make the text their own property, linking its components in their own preferred way.

This freedom of choice has its limits. If we just want to find out about Bram Stoker, we don't want to waste time on Bela Lugosi, even if the author thinks Lugosi is important. But most of the time, as readers, we expect the author to have mapped out our route for us, just as we expect a travel agent to plan details of our trip. We assume the travel agent knows more than we do and can anticipate our needs. Maybe we want some flexibility built into our itinerary, but we don't want to fly from New York to Paris, back to New York, and then to Frankfurt.

Pushed to a logical extreme, the hypertext author might as well hand the reader a set of Scrabble tiles and say: "Here, make your own text." But that's not authorship, any more than 52 Pickup is a card game. Our readers expect some kind of coherence in our hypertext. We can and should provide such coherence, but we should be aware of some specific challenges in doing so.

Hypertext is by definition nonlinear, but remember that "linearity" itself is just a metaphor for a one-at-a-time sequence — especially a sequence we're familiar with. The sequence A-B-C is "linear" only because that's the sequence we have learned. So is 1-2-3, and so is subject-verb-object. Because we've memorized certain patterns, we can expect D to follow C,

3 to follow 2, and verb (usually) to follow subject. When we put information into a numbered sequence, for example, we expect #1 to be more important or more basic than #2, because we're used to hearing important or introductory material before we hear details or complicated material that assumes we understand the basics.

In the rest of this book, I'll examine some of the problems — and opportunities — that hypertext offers to you as a Website writer.

As you develop content for your Website, you should bear in mind some basic facts about the medium.

Computer-Screen Text Is Hard to Read

You may not realize it but your monitor has awful resolution. Maybe the text looks crisp and sharp compared to that on those old green-on-black monitors of the mid-1980s. But take a look at your text on-screen and then at a laser printout. Once you look back at your screen, the text will be a sight for sore eyes, and you'll realize how difficult it is to read lots of text on-screen.

Studies in the 1980s, reported by Web analyst and usability advocate Jakob Nielsen, found that reading from a monitor is 25 percent slower than reading from printed paper.

This seems to result from the poor resolution of computer screens, and in 1998, Nielsen was reporting that expensive experimental monitors with very high resolution can bring reading speeds back up to normal. He predicts high-end users will have such screens by 2003, and all users by 2008.

For the time being, however, we're stuck trying to read text on low-resolution screens. We don't always consciously realize it, but reading 75 words of text from a computer monitor feels as long as reading 100 words on paper. Reading from a monitor is tiring in other ways as well: try reading this book while holding it straight out in front of you at arm's length. When your arms get tired, just prop it up at the same distance. It feels unnatural because it is unnatural. You'd rather hold the book in your lap, or on a tabletop within a foot of your eyes.

As a Distinguished Engineer at Sun Microsystems for many years, Jakob Nielsen was in an excellent position to observe the development of computer-displayed text. His Alertbox Website contains informative and thought-provoking essays and reports on the evolution of the Web. See his column "In Defense of Print" at <http://www.useit.com/alertbox/9602.html>.

See Jakob Nielsen's "The End of Legacy Media (Newspapers, Magazines, Books, TV Networks)" at <http://www.useit.com/alertbox/980823.html>.

To improve the readability of your text, you can provide lots of blank space around it, as you would in a résumé. This means limiting the amount of text you put on a single screen. You may choose to display your text in a column that reaches only halfway across the screen, leaving wide margins on either side or areas of blank space that provide respite for your readers' eyes. While this display may mean that on-screen readers will have to scroll down the page to read the full article, shortening the length of the lines makes text more readable. This is why newspapers display text in narrow columns.

Most Web authoring tools like Adobe GoLive or Microsoft Front Page should have no trouble importing word-processed files that are formatted with short line lengths and lots of blank space. If someone else is putting your text up on the Website, be sure you agree on a consistent and readable format for archived documents.

There are more tips on style and display throughout this book.

Readers, Not Authors, Determine Page Appearance

Web designer David Siegel's Website is at <http://www.dsiegel.com/home.html>.

People surfing the Web are using many different Web browsers and versions of those browsers. Some browsers can't deal with graphics at all, never mind plug-in applications like Java, Shockwave, and Real Audio that let your browser display special effects including digital video and sound. Even more people, I suspect, keep their browser's default display settings. In the case of Netscape, that means a dull gray background and a 12-point typeface. As sophisticated Web designers like David Siegel persuasively argue, this configuration is far from ergonomic. Such text is hard to read, so the impatient surfer goes somewhere else. The patient surfer stays, reads, and gets a headache.

Maybe you've got a font that improves text readability and looks great as well. If the people reading your Web page don't have that font on their computers, however, your text may appear in the default font of their browser. You can get around this by converting your text into a graphic — but that will take much longer to download, and some of your readers may not even have graphics ability on their computers and so they won't be able to read any parts of your message. You may present text in some dramatic format using a plug-in (a software application that works with your browser to create special effects) like Shockwave, but readers without the plug-in won't be able to see the text at all. (And if your readers do go to the trouble of finding and installing the plug-in, and then come back only to be disappointed with the actual content of what they can now see, don't expect them to visit your site again.)

So, like a World War II convoy, your speed and maneuverability depend on the abilities of your slowest reader. If you are interested in reaching only readers who have the latest plug-ins for the latest browser on the biggest, fastest new computer, fine. But you may sacrifice a lot of potential sales or job interviews or people who share your interests. In general, you should endeavor to make your technology serve your intended audience. That, of course, means knowing your audience, which I will discuss in the next two chapters.

2
STRUCTURING YOUR WEBSITE

As a Web author, you should be mentally organizing your material into hypertext. Maybe your readers won't choose to follow your organization, but if you visualize some kind of pattern for your material, it will at least make your own writing easier. If you understand the built-in problems of navigation and reader behavior, you can minimize their effects; throwing information into your Website at random because you know that "hypertext is nonlinear" will only make your Website chaotic.

Hypertext can be any length, from a single letter or numeral to the collected works of Tolstoy. But for ease of reading, a computer monitor should display the equivalent of only a third to a half of a page of double-spaced typescript — say about 100 words. You can, of course, pack much more than that into a single screen, but only if you reduce the point size of your type to illegibility and single-space the text. This is sure to drive your readers away: the eye recoils from unbroken masses of text, whether on a page or a screen.

You have just two choices for organizing your material: chunk it or scroll it. How you organize your material depends on the material itself and the uses your readers are likely to make of it. The Web is good for two kinds of information retrieval: hit and run, and downloading.

Chunking: Hit and Run Information Retrieval

Hit and run information retrieval is what most of us do when we surf the Web. We visit a site, see if anything looks interesting, click on it, get our jolt (or fail to get it), and go on to another site. Maybe we found nothing much or maybe the site changed our lives, but the information we retrieved was contained on one screen or less. The author had to present it as briefly and dramatically as possible so we would be interested in and understand it, and perhaps go on to other small chunks of information within his or her site. (Many Webwriters use the word "chunk" to describe whatever information you can fit on a single screen; we'll use the term in this way also.)

When chunking, you break your material up into segments of not more than 100 words (often much less), so that every word within a chunk is visible on a monitor screen. This pattern helps the reader to grasp all the information on the page. Two or more chunks, when linked electronically, form a stack. Links will take readers to other pages in the stack, often by several different pathways. However, some browsers are pretty slow at finding the next page in the hypertext stack, and your readers may desert you rather than wait around. You'd better make sure your first page provides plenty of reasons for readers to explore deeper into your stack. I'll discuss ways to do so in the next chapter. I'll also discuss ways to organize chunked text into clear hierarchies.

Hit and run retrieval means scanning short (screen-sized) passages of text and graphics. *Chunks* are screen-sized text passages usually no more than 100 words long. Two or more chunks, linked together, form a stack. Hit and run readers are looking for easily understood bits of information; chunks should be understandable without reference to other text passages.

Sound and Pictures Can Undercut Text

In the early days of television commercials, advertisers discovered to their horror that they were sabotaging themselves by using images so fantastic that viewers were distracted from the products being advertised. They already knew that viewers wanted jolts in the form of vivid and dramatic images, even if they were in black and white. However, only with huge budgets could advertisers afford to feed that appetite.

What's more, advertisers felt they had to outdo their competitors, who were also trying to stop viewers from heading for the bathroom during the commercial breaks. So advertising was filled with wild and wonderful images that would command attention.

But when advertisers did follow-up interviews and market research, they learned that consumers rarely connected the fantastic images on the screen with the products that the images were supposed to help sell. The images were actually making people tune out the message.

Rosser Reeves, a 1950s advertising guru, called this effect "vampire video." Once he'd understood and named the problem, his commercials didn't abandon graphics, but the images became strictly subordinate to the message. Sometimes they were even the message itself: if viewers turned off the sound, they still got the sales pitch delivered as on-screen text. Reeves's ads passed the critical test: people got the message and bought the product.

The Web is now in a stage comparable to 1950s television advertising and 1980s computer design. Remember when computers began to offer simple graphics and a choice of fonts? Remember the cluttered documents people produced, with several fonts per page, plus Dingbats and clipart as far as the eye could see? Website creators are doing awful things with graphics and audio, partly because they can and partly because they don't yet know they shouldn't.

Your choices as a Web author will depend on the relative importance of text and graphics on your Website. If you're a graphic artist displaying your work, your text will be minimal, even nonexistent. If text is critical, then bells and whistles should appear only when they enhance the message (that is, make it more understandable, more surprising, more persuasive) or make reading it easier and more interesting.

Scrolling: Information Retrieval by Downloading

Downloading retrieval means obtaining from a Website a long archived document (even a book-length one), often including graphics, which readers will print out or read on the screen.

An *archived document* is usually one originally written for text on paper, which is stored electronically so readers can download it and print out their own copies.

Technical writer Michael Hoffman makes a very strong case for scrolling text — with detailed tables of contents and internal links — in his article "Enabling Extremely Rapid Navigation in Your Web or Document," at <http://www.pdrinterleaf.com/infoaxcs.htm>.

Sometimes readers surf for very detailed information online — perhaps a government report or a long news story, or maybe even a whole book. It would be pointless to break up such texts into independent chunks to be read in any order; the original authors intended them to be read in a certain sequence, with all the usual navigation cues of linear text printed on paper. However, the text may be too long to fit on the screen all at once, so the reader must scroll through such documents.

Long, linear-text documents really belong back on paper, however, and your Website is just an archive for them. You don't need to worry quite as much about brevity with these documents; readers who want to scrutinize them and not just scan them can download them to their hard drives and then print them out in whatever format they prefer.

However, many visitors to your Website will read at least part of such an archive on the monitor, whatever the cost in slowed reading speed and eyestrain. Scrolling tires out most readers very quickly, so if you choose to use it, provide internal links, such as a list of keyword links at the top of the file. Clicking on a link will take readers directly to the section of interest, enabling them to rappel like rock climbers down the text. When they're through reading a particular section, they can jump back to the top to find something else. A list of keywords also provides a useful overview of the text's main parts. For details on navigation, see Chapter 3.

You can also make reading long archived texts online easier with a few simple adjustments to the layout of the text. If you display your text in a column about half the width of your screen, each line will be only about 10 or 12 words long. Most people find this to be a comfortable line length to read, although, of course, it means still more scrolling. Unlike with text chunks (see above), as a general rule, you should single-space archived documents, with a double space between paragraphs. That makes paragraph indentations unnecessary, and gives your readers a welcome patch of white space between paragraphs to make reading easier. Without such breaks, readers get lost in a mass of text.

▶　▶　▶

When determining whether to chunk or scroll your text, you're not facing a clear-cut decision between a "bad" design (long, scrolling text) and a "good" one (chunks of text): Both have their uses. As a writer, you must decide whether your material is more useful in chunks written for hit and run readers, or in scrolling text meant to be printed out on paper. Whether you're writing for the hit and run reader or the downloader, you should be presenting text that's as clear, brief, and useful as you can make it.

The Three Principles of Webtext

You may intend your Website to be simply an electronic archive of writing designed for text on paper. Or you may be using hypertext in avant-garde literary experiments for small audiences. In such cases, you can happily ignore the advice that follows. Otherwise, whatever the purpose and content of your site, I suggest that your text should reflect three basic principles: Orientation, Information, and Action.

In a business letter, for example, you supply appropriate background information and standard formatting (Orientation) to help the reader make sense of your main message (Information) and to understand what should happen as a result of that information (Action). So you might explain that overcrowding in your warehouse is forcing you to offer widgets at unheard-of low prices, and customers can act on that information by calling your toll-free telephone number.

These principles operate very similarly in Webtext.

Orientation

When your readers arrive at your site, they need two kinds of orientation: background knowledge about the site, and navigation aids to help them get around the site. So the front page of your site should orient your readers by telling them —

- what the site's about,
- how it's organized, and
- how to navigate it.

Sometimes the title of the site tells visitors what it's about:

> Your Guide to Chesterton

Often, however, you may need a few lines of explanation:

> The complete directory of Chesterton's tourist attractions, businesses, and municipal services.

You may also need to elaborate on your organizational principle:

> This site consists of six main pages: <u>Tourist Attractions</u>, <u>Lodging</u>, <u>Dining</u>, <u>Business Guide</u>, <u>Municipal Services</u>, and <u>Community News</u>.

Or you may present those topics as a set of buttons or graphics. You may want to offer more direct links from the front page by making it look more like a table of contents:

> <u>Municipal Services</u>
>
> > <u>City Hall</u>
> >
> > <u>Police</u>
> >
> > <u>Parks Department</u>
> >
> > <u>School Board</u>
> >
> > <u>Highways Office</u>
> >
> > <u>Hospital</u>

I discuss navigation cues such as the table of contents and navigation buttons in more detail in Chapter 3.

In judging the effectiveness of your orientation, you can apply two secondary principles: Minimalism and Coherence.

Minimalism

Is the orientation you are supplying the least the reader needs? If you're tempted to begin an orienting statement with, "As you probably know," you can probably drop the statement altogether. Minimalism also means you shouldn't put too many items on your site. Every item may potentially add to the reader's navigation problems, so be sure that each one has a good reason for being there. Sometimes a link to another site is all you need.

Coherence

Does a given chunk of text make sense on its own? If it deals with two or three ideas in 100 words or so, do you supply clear transitions from one idea to the next? Does this chunk behave like other chunks on your site? For example, suppose you have a chunk describing a local hotel, with a link to nearby restaurants; will other "lodging" chunks also link in the same way to restaurants? Once your readers understand your navigation system, they will expect to use it throughout your site, so you should endeavor to be consistent.

Don't forget that since many readers may first come to your site through a page other than your front page, orientation is important on every single page of your Website. But it need not always be quite as detailed as on your front page.

Information

Your site provides readers with information in the form of text and graphics, whether displayed on several linked pages or on one long, scrolling page. Whatever that information may include, two secondary principles are at work here: Clarity and Correctness.

Clarity

Your text should be understandable at first glance, even to readers with little formal education or from a different cultural background. If readers must puzzle over unfamiliar or ambiguous words, you are making them work harder than they need to. This is true even if your site deals with a specialist topic. For example, maybe you've created a site about extensible markup language (XML), which is a way of writing code for Websites that require highly technical information; are you using long and complicated words just because you can, where shorter ones would really be more clear and straightforward? Even your expert readers deserve the simplest, clearest discussion you can provide.

Correctness

On one level, "correctness" means basics such as proper spelling, good grammar, and accurate names and addresses. This kind of correctness is also part of clarity because it helps readers understand your message more easily.

But every message has two components, verbal and nonverbal, and if they're in conflict, readers tend to trust the nonverbal message. Spelling or grammatical errors on, say, a lawyer's Website will send a nonverbal message about the lawyer's poor attention to detail. Any professional or business Website must convey a nonverbal message of competence; errors in language basics and errors of fact undercut that message.

Action

What action do you want your readers to take as a result of absorbing the information on your Website? Should they email you, provide a credit-card number, subscribe to a listserv, or click on the link to your advertisers? If you are going to get the results you want, you need to consider two secondary principles: A positive attitude and the "you" attitude.

A positive attitude

Even if your site is denouncing violations of human rights or the destruction of the environment, you must think your users can do something about those problems. Otherwise, why bother to create a site? So, when you present problems, suggested solutions should be close at hand: documents with important information, links to groups with political influence, or email addresses of powerful people.

The "you" attitude

Webwriting should present facts and ideas in terms of the reader's advantage. So be sure to talk more about your reader than about yourself. Instead of writing:

> I've listed the top 15 companies I consider a threat to the environment.

— you can write:

> You can email your protests to the top 15 environmental pol-
> luters.

This is more than simple courtesy. Your readers have their own purposes for coming to your site, and you are there to serve those purposes. If
you understand what your readers want and you anticipate their needs, your
site will succeed and your readers will return.

Consideration is an important part of the nonverbal message that conveys the "you" attitude. Your readers are doing you a favor by visiting your
site, and you owe them a rewarding experience. Will they stick around for
that killer graphic to download if they've only got a 14.4 Kbps modem?
Will they really want to scroll through your list of the 100 worst movies of
all time? Will they follow one of your links to a File Not Found message?
An out-of-date site with "link rot" (links that go nowhere) wastes readers'
time.

So put yourself in your readers' shoes: If you were a stranger arriving
at your own site, would you feel as if the site's creator had made a special
effort to make life easy for you?

If we accept these three principles of Webwriting, several useful guidelines
for structuring content emerge from them. These are discussed in detail in
the next chapter.

3
ORGANIZING WEBSITE CONTENT

Orientation: Navigation Cues

Provide readers with a site overview

Robert E. Horn, in his book *Mapping Hypertext,* points out that linear text is full of cues that help the reader navigate. Organization of print text is hierarchical, for example. We expect each section to include some general statement or thesis, supported by various kinds of evidence or illustration. We start a book with an overview or introduction that summarizes important points, and we often find that chapters of the book feature similar introductions. In hypertext, says Horn, we need to present the whole hierarchy of the text in some kind of overview, such as a navigation bar whose buttons will take us to different sections within the text.

Your front page may include a big headline and a summary about the purpose of the site, but it should essentially be a table of contents. You can organize your hypertext in a number of ways, including —

- alphabetically,
- numerically,
- chronologically,

Present an Overview
Readers may try to mentally organize hypertext into some kind of hierarchy, but that may not be easy; Web expert Robert E. Horn suggests that some kind of overview always be visible.

- graphically, or
- completely at random (which I don't recommend).

A list of employees' telephone numbers and email addresses would naturally be alphabetical — probably just a string of letter-links (A, B, C, etc.) across the screen. So would a list of departments within your organization. A sequence describing a process in time might be a numbered list; so might a categorical list of topics running from most important to least important.

Many Websites use graphical contents pages. These can range from something as simple as an organizational chart to an elaborate map full of graphic cues: a cartoon of a policeman in a kiosk, for example, linking to the name and telephone number of the company's security officer. Be careful when using graphical cues in the place of textual ones as many new Web users may not recognize the cartoon as a link, which will defeat its purpose.

If you're confident that your graphics are intuitive and self-explanatory to anyone from any cultural or educational background, you don't have to worry about refining the text on your contents page. Otherwise, you should try to make your text as clear as possible, even if it seems redundant to those who do understand the graphics.

A pop song of yesteryear might be the anthem of Webwriters: "Shut the door, they're coming in the window." Web surfers can directly access just about any page on your site that doesn't require a password. You can create a detailed, well-organized front page with a clear statement of your site's purpose and a good table of contents, but if I ask a search engine to find pages that mention snowboarding, and one of your other pages features the word "snowboarding," I will go to that page without ever seeing the rest of your site, let alone your front page. I won't even know much about your site unless you give me information and navigation aids on your snowboarding page.

Every page on your site should at least have a link to your front page or display a table of contents, so your readers who have entered your site "through the window" will at least know where they are and what else your site has to offer. The terms you use in the table of contents should be identical to the headings you have used in the text. Your readers want to find their way around your site with the least possible hassle. If each page has consistent, clear navigation guides, readers will be grateful.

Many sites are now offering not only a table of contents, but an index page that provides a direct link to each individual page on the site. An index page may not have room for blurbs, but it's a good idea to group pages into sections. So if your Website on the town of Chesterton has a page for each hotel in Chesterton, list those pages in the index under a section on Lodging — not in alphabetical order by hotel name interspersed with all the other index entries.

You may want to create a "frames" page, in which the screen is subdivided into two or more windows. One window may offer your table of contents as a list of links; click on a link and it displays in the main window. The advantage of this is that your table of contents is always visible and readers don't have to scroll to the top or bottom of your site to access it. Many people dislike frames, however, or still don't have browsers that can display them. Some people also are unable to print hard copies of frames pages. You can still provide some basic links on each page by creating a page template with those links built in. (Most Web authoring programs will let you create frames and templates when you start to create pages.)

Signal transitions with navigation buttons

In print text, paragraph indentations signal new topics or subtopics, punctuation marks define relationships between words and phrases, and transition words and phrases (e.g., Meanwhile, Secondly, Nevertheless, A day later, Another argument) let readers know how each paragraph connects to the previous one. In hypertext, such transitions are generally meaningless because readers may jump from section to section in various sequences.

Linear text often prepares us for sequences:

Your journey to Mexico will include stays in Cuernavaca, Puebla, and Acapulco.

When we read sentences like this one, we expect descriptions of each Mexican city. Hypertext can prepare us for such sequences only by some cue outside the sequence, such as navigation buttons labeled <u>Cuernavaca</u>, <u>Puebla</u>, and <u>Acapulco</u>.

See Jakob Nielsen's Alertbox essay "How Users Read on the Web" at <http://www.useit.com/alertbox/9710a.html>.

Your front page may include not only links to sections of the site but also links to different passages within a single page — especially if it's a long, scrolling page. This allows readers to skip up and down the page to the paragraphs they're most interested in.

Be careful about the directional terms you use to label your navigation buttons since your readers aren't all arriving at your site via your front page. If readers arrive via AltaVista, Hotbot, or some other search engine, and land on your Puebla page, a navigation link that says Back to Home Page doesn't make much sense. How can they go "back" to some place they've never been? Why have a button that says Next if the page it links to has nothing to do with Puebla? It would be better to create navigation links that say To Mexico Home Page or To Acapulco Page.

If you are working with long, scrolling documents, provide ways to jump to the beginning and various sections of the document at the bottom of the page, and perhaps at intermediate stages:

To Top of Financial Aid Page

To Chesterton College Policies Page

To Chesterton College Home Page

Your readers may bring some print-media habits with them. If so, they'll assume that any items listed near the top of the Web page are either introductory material or the most important material on the page. They may also scan from left to right and then pay most attention to whatever is in the upper righthand corner — very much as we do when we scan a newspaper's front page. If you would rather direct readers to some other part of the page, you may need to spell out your preferred sequence: Read Me First, Introduction, If You're New to This Site…, or some such cue.

Orientation: Headlines

Headlines can include the title of your site, the titles of individual pages, and subheadings that break up text. Like the thesis sentence of a paragraph, headlines tell readers what to expect, so they deserve some thought before you write them.

Ideally, the title of your site should tell readers what it's about: In Praise of Holly Cole, or Your Guide to Chesterton. Many of your readers will find you through a search engine that gives them the site title and the first few words of text. If your title is Paradise! and your introductory text is "Here is the land the conquistadors sought…," readers searching for Chesterton may not realize this is the site they've been looking for.

If you're skilled in HTML, you can write a meta-tag that some search engines will display instead of the first few words on your page. A keyword meta-tag lists words and phrases that searchers might use: skiing, snowboarding, winter sports, hiking, alpine environment, recreation. Some sites load such keywords (invisibly) onto their front pages so that search engines will display the sites in the first batch of "hits" the engines turn up. Many search engines, however, will reject sites with lists of meta-tags; if they find the word "skiing" repeated ten times in an invisible meta-tag, the engines recognize that this is an attempt to get the site to the top of the list of hits, and will not display the site.

If you don't know how to create meta-tags, don't worry. Just make sure the keywords that readers are likely to search for are in your title and first few lines of text. Search engines will usually include those lines in their lists of hits. If the first text on your site is just the titles of your navigation buttons — Home, News Releases, President's Message — readers won't have much sense of what's really on your site, so they may not take a chance on visiting it.

How you display your title headline is also important. If you've turned it into a huge graphic that takes a long time to download, some impatient visitors may leave before they see it. Others will wait, only to be disappointed that it's just your company logo, or a photograph of you with your name in 3D letters. Better to keep your title as regular text, in a legible font.

Keep your headlines close to the text they introduce. Usually, headlines, including subheads, should be just one double space from the first line of regular text that follows.

Use subheads

Subheads can greatly help your readers. If you're writing and organizing your text in screen-size chunks, subheads will prepare readers for the content that is to appear in the following chunk. You may even find that a single chunk of 100 words can still benefit from two or three subheads.

If you're providing long, scrolling text, subheads will help to break it up into manageable lengths. If the document is over 1,000 words long, break it up with subheads, and create links to those subheads at the top of the page:

Financial Aid and Awards

General Information   Services of the   Publications
                        Financial Aid Office

Scholastic Awards   Deadlines for   Emergency Funding
                        Applications

Your readers now have the choice of scrolling through the whole section, or jumping to particular sections of interest.

Hook readers' interest:
Hooks, links, and blurbs

For a word less than 100 years old, "blurb" has gone through some remarkable changes in meaning.

American humorist Gelett Burgess coined the term in 1907. He sketched a voluptuous blonde as cover art for a book jacket, and named her "Miss Blinda Blurb." For some time, sexy cover art was a blurb, but the word also came to mean any overdone praise of a book appearing on the jacket.

While that's still an accepted meaning, the pulp magazines of the 1920s and 1930s picked it up in a different sense — the brief summary of a story appearing between the title and the text. Its purpose was to tempt readers into investing the time to read the story.

On the Web, we now use "blurb" to mean a notice about what to expect on the other side of a link. Like the pulp magazines, we want our readers to make that jump and invest some time in our text. They're more likely to if they have a sense of what they're getting themselves into. Without that sense, they may be reluctant to wander into the labyrinth. In effect, we haven't given them adequate orientation for our site.

A good link should have two parts, though they may appear in a single word or phrase: a hook and a blurb. The hook — a term borrowed from magazine writing — is something at the beginning of a text that grabs reader attention. In our case, the hook is usually the text of the link itself: <u>Best Snowboarding in Colorado</u>, or <u>Typical House Prices in Lynn Valley</u>. If you think that's enough to draw readers through the link, then fine. Bear in mind that you have a wide range of hooking devices to choose from:

- **Quotation Marks.** "We love to read text that someone is supposed to have actually spoken," says Crawford Kilian.

- **Question.** A question promises an answer, and we'll jump through the link to find it.

- **Unusual statement.** Anything surprising will give the reader a jolt and wonder what other bizarre things you may have to say.

- **Comparison/contrast.** Comparisons show how things are similar; contrasts show how they differ.

- **News peg.** A tie-in with some big current event can draw interest (but don't let the news peg go stale on you).

- **Promise of conflict.** An attack or refutation makes us want to read more.

- **Direct address.** Web writing needs the "you" attitude, so talk right to the reader.

These hooks may stand on their own, but sometimes you're trapped with text that may be confusing or ambiguous. I teach in a Communications department, and I get a lot of mail intended for our public-relations people (who work in what's called "college relations"). What if you're trying to show the difference between your company's Information Systems department and your Information Services department? That's where a blurb comes in handy:

<u>Information Systems</u>

Computer support, Webmaster, staff training.

Information Services

Public relations, technical editing, company newsletter, advertising purchases.

Even if your text link seems self-explanatory, a blurb may make it more inviting. Maybe your text link is <u>What makes a good business plan?</u> The implied promise of an answer becomes more explicit with a blurb like: "Six successful entrepreneurs offer practical advice."

Whatever hook you use, make sure it's appropriate. A promise of conflict, for example, had better deliver the conflict.

You can also make life easier for your readers by turning both hook and blurb into links. Suppose you have a link to <u>Company Personnel Policies</u>. Make the jump and you find yourself on a page full of still more links. Give readers the chance to go directly to the policy they want:

Company Personnel Policies

Policies dealing with <u>Hiring</u>, <u>Probationary Period</u>, <u>Employee Evaluation Procedures</u>, <u>Health & Safety Issues</u>, <u>Conflict Resolution</u>, <u>Salary Scale</u>, etc.

If screen space permits, you can break the blurb into a bulleted list or columns; the point is still to guide readers where they want to go, as quickly and conveniently as possible.

Fight the urge to turn the blurb into a mini-essay of its own. The blurb should always be the least you can possibly do. If the word, phrase, or sentence enables readers to use the link confidently, it's done its job.

The blurb might also indicate whether the text on the other side is an archive (a text originally written for print on paper) or a chunk (a text of no more than 80 or 100 words designed for "hit and run" reading). Many news sites do this when they display a headline and the first paragraph of a story, with (<u>Full Story</u>) at the end. You might do this with your company's annual report, with a summary in chunk form and the blurbs <u>Full Text in PDF</u> and <u>Full Text in HTML</u> as links.

With a link to chunked text, the blurb can simply make the link more explicit (again guiding readers where they want to go):

<u>Student Tuition Fees</u>

Fees for the 2000-2001 academic year for <u>resident</u> and <u>international</u> students.

Whatever page your readers land on, they should have the opportunity to respond to what they find — and to you. An email link may seem self-evident, but it might get more traffic with a blurb:

<u>ckilian@thehub.capcollege.bc.ca</u>
I'd love to hear your opinion of this advice!

Information

Analyze your audience

How you structure your site and what content you create should reflect the readers you want to attract to your site, and why. Are you looking for customers, converts, students, employers, kindred spirits? Are they experienced in using the Web, or complete novices? Do they speak English? Do they read it?

In some cases, you can draw a detailed demographic analysis based on careful research: maybe you're trying to sell package tours to singles aged 18 to 34, or providing medical advice for parents of children with cystic fibrosis, or celebrating a pop singer who appeals to girls aged 13 to 17. Much of what you have to say — in both content and style — should reflect what you know about that readership.

In other cases, your subject will cross boundaries of age, gender, and nationality. Your audience will care about the research you've put into the subject, but it would be impossible to do similar research into the audience itself. This is where research yields to soul search: you have to ask yourself what other fans of Holly Cole would really like to find on your site, or what information would excite potential applicants to your college's computer-animation program.

Whatever decisions you make about the nature of your desired audience, don't forget that many in that target group simply don't have access to the Web, or don't even know about your site. Meanwhile, many other people who are not among your desired audience may turn up out of curiosity or by accident. Presumably you want them to leave with a good impression of you, your organization, and your intended audience, even if they're not especially interested in the subject of your site. So even if your site is highly specialized, it should offer something to the casual visitor.

Organize consciously

Don't throw material into your site at random, just because it's hypertext. You have several possible ways to organize your content.

Narrative order

Narrative order involves describing a process through time. If it's a fairly extended narrative (e.g., My Six Months Backpacking Through Africa), you might as well make it a single long document and treat it as a downloadable archive. If it's a short narrative, or breaks logically into subsections, it might work better in chunks. For example, if you're describing the process of home brewing, each stage might get its own page. Readers can go to the page they're interested in without having to scroll through material they don't want. However, readers may want to print out the text explaining the whole process, so you could make it available as a single document elsewhere on your site. (Be sure to let readers know that it's available.)

Logical order

When you present text in logical order, you make an assertion, you bring in your documentation to back it up, and you come to a conclusion. This may get long-winded, so your arguments are likely to end up at archive length rather than in short, powerful chunks.

If you're really familiar with the Web, you may be tempted to simply mention your sources and turn them into links:

Web designer Jeffrey Zeldman defines three kinds of audiences on the Web:

Viewers look for audiovisual entertainment. They like splashy graphics, exciting sounds, and quick jolts. Viewers treat the Web like radio, TV, or movies, and don't have much use for text except as directions to the next surprise.

Users look for information that they can apply to their own work. For example, they might want to use your statistics in their report or follow your model in composing a business plan. Users love hit-and-run retrieval.

Readers actually sit and scroll through long documents (or print them out to read on paper). Readers may read for entertainment or for use, but they're not in a hurry. Readers love archives.

A famous American scientist, <u>Linus Pauling</u>, started the modern craze for vitamin C as a cure-all.

If you do this, however, your readers may surf away to the Linus Pauling Home Page and may not return to your site. A more useful approach for citing sources is to put your links to sources at the end of your argument. That way, readers will finish reading your argument and then visit your sources if they are interested.

Categorical order

Hypertext comes into its own when text is organized in categorical order. You have a subject that breaks more or less obviously into chunks, with no particular reason to list chunks in a specific order. To spare your readers from navigation problems and information overload, you have to impose some kind of order on your categorical material. Maybe your site has a page with links to five other pages describing the five most popular trails in your regional park. You could list them from shortest to longest (or vice versa), from north to south, from easiest to hardest, even in alphabetical order. The blurb on the front page could indicate how you've organized them, from shortest to longest, for example:

<u>Alpine Meadows Trail</u>. 6 km. Really steep, but what views!

<u>High Corniche Trail</u>. 18 km. For experienced hikers only.

Readers will simply use your blurb as a guide to the trails that most interest them.

If you're simply transferring a print document (like a company report or a park brochure) to a Website, imposing categorical order on your material will not be an issue. But if you're generating your own text, you may feel baffled trying to sort it all out. You want to present coherent, easy-to-follow text, but your mind operates like simmering minestrone soup: ideas float to the surface, then sink again. Try to force organization on your own thoughts, and you get the cerebral equivalent of a system crash.

Clustering is one effective way to begin ordering your material. It's a simple process for outwitting yourself. Let the ideas of possible topics to include on your Website come into your head in whatever order they like,

Put your links to sources at the end of your text so that readers don't surf away to another site and never return to yours.

27

Create a Hierarchy

Hypertext layout may mislead readers by emphasizing the wrong details. Jakob Nielsen points out that Web readers tend to scan the screen, rather than read every word, so they may well miss an important fact, or give too much weight to a minor one placed in a prominent, scannable position.

You need to ensure that readers' attention goes to your key points. Therefore, your key points should appear in the first lines of a section, where they automatically assume importance. Minor points can go into the same section, but be buried inside the text — the famous inverted pyramid structure of a newspaper story.

Here's an example of a page organized to emphasize the key items first:
Our product line includes <u>running shoes</u>, <u>walking shoes</u>, and <u>hiking boots</u>
or
Our product line includes:
<u>running shoes</u>
<u>walking shoes</u>
<u>hiking boots</u>.

Before readers click on the first underlined link, they know what categories they're dealing with.

and jot them down as they occur to you. One idea inspires another; write that down too. Eventually you have several sheets of paper (or a computer screen) covered with ideas in no particular sequence.

Now that those ideas are out of your head, you can look at them and see which belong with which. Some are clearly introductory; others deal with the main subject; still others are part of the conclusion. Cluster these ideas by tagging all the introductory items with a #1 or an A. The central ideas could be tagged #2, #3, #4, or B, C, D; the concluding ideas, #5 or E. If you're doing this exercise with one of the newer word processors, you can drag the ideas into the appropriate clusters using the word processor's outlining function, and before you know it you're organized.

Suppose you're putting together the Website for Chesterton, a year-round sports and sightseeing destination. You might start jotting down ideas something like this:

> history, skiing, snowboarding, zinc mine, logging, motels, hotels, youth hostels, regional parks, shopping, wildlife, environmental problems, swimming, waterskiing, hiking trails, entertainment, restaurants

Obviously, some ideas inspired related ones, but most topics just occurred to you more or less at random. You see some obvious categories: Winter Sports, Summer Sports, Lodging. In the Winter Sports category, you could put skiing and snowboarding — and, come to think of it, you can also put in something about snowshoeing and ice skating.

Later on, you may want a separate page for Winter Sports, or you may decide to lump them in with other activities in a Year-Round Sports section.

Clustering works for almost any kind of writing task, and in Webwriting it also suggests how you might design your navigation system. Maybe each section of your text will have its own navigation button on your front page. Or, if you're creating a long, scrolling page, a contents list at the top of the page could provide links to each section.

Style and Display

You should be generating your Webtext in whatever font and size are comfortable for you. You know that your readers may have set their machines to display some other default font, in some other size, and you can't control that. You also know that PCs and Macs may display your site somewhat differently. But you can ensure that your readers at least come close to seeing your text as you wish them to.

First, bear in mind that a serif font, like the one used in the main text of this book, is usually easier to read in extended text than a sans serif font, like the one used for headings throughout this book. So if you have long passages of text, a serif font is your best bet. Point size makes a difference too. Usually, type should appear at no smaller than 10 points and no larger than 14 points. Readers with poor eyesight especially will prefer larger point sizes.

Stick with plain text. Use capital letters, small caps, italics, and boldface sparingly. The purpose of these special displays is to emphasize something; the more displays you use, the less emphasis anything will get. A whole paragraph in italics or small caps or regular caps will be difficult to read. Combining special displays only makes matters worse. A headline in ***BOLD ITALIC CAPS*** is overkill. If you must use all-uppercase letters, scale down the point size a little. And don't even think about underlining for emphasis; on the Web, an underline means a link.

Remember that a font like Georgia in 12-point is great for reading on a monitor but may be awkward as a printer font. For example, a table may not print completely because 12-point Georgia makes the table too big to fit on a letter-sized page.

A Web author can specify a particular font and size right in the HTML code of the site. As long as the font is one that readers have on their computers, the site will appear more or less as the author wants it to. But if the font isn't there, the reader's default font will take over anyway — perhaps with disastrous results for display and readability. You should probably leave decisions about display up to your readers.

Be very careful about mixing colors. If you choose a black background and then display text in dark blue, you are going to make your site unreadable. The same is true of light colors, such as yellow text on a pale-green background. Good old black text on a white page should serve you well for most purposes. Your Web authoring program will usually let you specify the colors you want for your text and background.

Unless you intend your archived material to be printed out rather than read off the screen, try to avoid running text the full width of the monitor. A column about half the width of the screen is much easier to read because no line will be much more than ten words long. Any longer, and readers will have trouble finding the beginning of the next line.

Formatting for printing

Bear in mind that your readers may want to use your text both on-screen and on paper. Anyone who has tried printing from the screen, however, finds that not all documents look the same on paper. If you intend or expect your text to be used in both media, you can make readers' lives easier by avoiding certain practices:

- A wide multicolumned table can pack a lot of information into a single screen, but the reader's printer may not pick up the whole table (especially if the browser is set to display a big screen font and the reader hasn't remembered to switch to a printer font).

- Sidebars and frames can look ghastly and make the text almost unusable; readers eventually learn the command "print frame," but why force them to if you can avoid it?

- Hyphenated words can make your screen text look tidy, but the hyphens may carry over into reformatted print text, where they become needless errors. The solution in most cases is simply to use a ragged-right margin with no hyphenations at all.

- Page number references usually become meaningless once a Web page is printed out, as do navigation cues such as Next and Back.

When you are organizing your information and text, keep your readers in mind. If you know your site will get mostly hit and run readers, your pages will have to display concise chunks of text. If you're planning a "library" of long documents for readers looking for detailed information, then you won't have to edit yourself quite as harshly. You will also have to consider how you want readers to respond to a particular item: with a click to some other chunk, or with an email answer? And will they get a suitable reward for their trouble? Webwriting, like chess, means you have to think several moves ahead — and put yourself in your readers' shoes.

Use bulleted lists

As readers, we're used to sentences on paper with long lists of nouns, verbs, and phrases. On the monitor such sentences become harder to read — and harder to respond to. This can be a problem in an interactive medium such as the Web.

Compare the following paragraph, taken from the next chapter, with its bulleted form:

The media have given us some of their own occupational slang, like "sound bite," but trendy clichés usually come from the occupations and professions most interesting to the chattering classes. So business has given us bottom lines, deep pockets, and downsizing. The military has given us bite the bullet, in the trenches, breakthrough, and flak. Engineering gives us parameters, state of the art, leading edge, and reinventing the wheel. Athletics gives us team players, ballpark figures, level playing fields, and track records. Politics is the home of charisma, spin doctors, bandwagons, and momentum. The self-help movement takes us from trendy clichés to what many consider outright psychobabble: self-actualizing, holistic, meaningful, one day at a time, and wellness.

The media have given us some of their own occupational slang, like "sound bite," but trendy clichés usually come from the occupations and professions most studied by the chattering classes:

- *Business:* bottom lines, deep pockets, downsizing
- *Military:* bite the bullet, in the trenches, breakthrough, flak
- *Engineering:* parameters, state of the art, leading edge, reinventing the wheel
- *Athletics:* team players, ballpark figures, level playing fields, track records
- *Politics:* charisma, spin doctors, bandwagons, momentum
- *Self-help movement:* self-actualizing, holistic, meaningful, one day at a time, wellness

Bulleted lists offer a couple of other advantages: You don't have to keep finding different ways to say the same thing (Business has given us, The military has given us, Athletics gives us), and it's easier to sound objective. In a bulleted list, my snide remark about "psychobabble" in the self-help movement has no place.

Bulleted lists might introduce a longer discussion of the topics mentioned, or might provide links to other sites dealing with the topics.

Action

Communication runs both ways

Fifty years ago, electronics engineers developed models of communication using "postal" and "projectile" metaphors: The message was like a package that must be delivered intact. (In 1999, FedEx commercials featured a horseman carrying a parcel through rivers and past gunmen, and triumphantly delivering it to a pioneer family.) The model assumes that the receiver understands the message and can accept and interpret it as easily — and passively — as your computer downloads a file.

These metaphors are unfortunately still common in business and education. Teachers still "deliver" courses like so much junk mail, while politicians and businesses "target" voters and consumers with messages that "get through" like armor-piercing bullets. Governments launch cruise missiles at other governments to "send a message." The basic premise is that communication is a monologue, valuable only to the extent that it creates the desired effect. Such models have been called "instrumental," since they treat communication as a tool for manipulating a passive receiver.

More sophisticated models treat communication not as a one-way missile launched at a passive target, but as a simultaneous two-way process in which participants constantly change their messages as they see how other participants are responding. This is the "inter" in "interactivity." Such models are called "constructive" because participants are actually creating meaning out of their exchanges.

If you design your Website as a missile-launching platform aimed at passive readers, you're missing the whole point of the Web. No matter what you put on your site, it's worthless until readers arrive, construe your meaning, and act on your information (assuming you've made it possible for them to act). Your readers, not you, will decide what your site really means and what value it has. You in turn have to respond to what your readers tell you, and before you know it, you're engaged in a conversation. If you listen to them and respond by adapting your content, you too are being interactive.

If you don't listen and don't adapt, your site is just a waste of time and bandwidth.

Response cues

Since the Web is supposed to be an interactive medium, your readers should respond to the information you provide with more than "So what?" You want them to take action.

Often, the only action needed for readers is to follow a link to another page, so the only response cue you need to provide is a clear link title and perhaps a blurb. But you may also want a more specific response: an email message, the submission of a form, a purchase order.

As marketers in the print media know, many people are slow and reluctant to respond on paper: they have to find a pen, and then an envelope, and then a stamp, and then they have to go out in the rain and mail their response. This is why so many companies provide stamped envelopes and some kind of bribe or threat — all simply to prod customers to respond.

Response is far easier on the Web. Click on an email address and an email form pops up; just type in a few words, click on the Send button, and you're done. If typing is too much trouble, just reply to questions by clicking on the buttons of a form. Worried about transmitting your credit card number over the Web? Just provide your telephone number, and the organization you want to order from will call you.

Easy as response may be, most Web users still don't respond — especially if it means spending money. We'll look at marketing in more detail in Chapter 8, but for now, let's just put ourselves in the readers' shoes. What's in it for them if they email you, fill out your form, join your listserv, or answer your questionnaire? Presumably there's some sort of reward, a benefit or pleasure they would otherwise miss out on. And they have to know they'll miss it!

So invite your readers to act in their own interest:

Just fill out this form to make sure you get regular updates on Holly Cole's concert tour — *plus* a chance to win a copy of her latest CD!

To reserve your beautiful room at Chesterton Lodge — at 10 percent off season rates — just send us your telephone number and we'll call right back to get your credit-card number and confirm your reservation.

If you want current news about the market for romances, you'll be glad you joined HEARTMART-L, the listserv for professional and aspiring romance novelists. All you need to do is send us an email, and market news and tips will start arriving within hours!

Do your symptoms point to a yeast infection as the cause of your feeling ill? Take this quick quiz simply by clicking on the Yes or No buttons after each question.

You can make a difference! Let your government representatives know what you think by adding your name to our email protest. They'll know in minutes that you're angry and you want results!

Notice that each invitation tries to make action sound effortless: Just fill out this form, All you need to do, They'll know in minutes. The action needed is built right into the appeal through a link to the suitable form. The Web is a culture of impatience, so effective appeals offer quick and painless ways to respond.

Reviewing a Website

We usually understand a problem better (and find solutions faster) when we can discuss it in detail. If you look at your Webtext in progress and all you can say is "This sucks!" you're not likely to improve it until you can identify the problem.

Reviewing someone else's site can help. The purpose of a Website review is to enable you to identify the key elements of a site (both concept and execution) and, thereby, to identify what may help or hurt your own site.

You may prefer to judge sites by the criteria discussed in:

- Jutta Degener's Dangerous Words:
  <http://kbs.cs.tu-berlin.de/%7Ejutta/ht/writing/words.html>

- Web Pages that Suck: <http://webpagesthatsuck.com>

- Worst of the Web: <http://www.worstoftheweb.com/>

Or you may want to develop your own criteria; if so, they may include some or all of the following:

- *Purpose.* Entertainment, marketing, information, or education? Is the purpose achieved? How? If not, why not — has the author misjudged the audience or misunderstood the nature and conventions of the Web?

- *Audience.* Novice or experienced? Young or old? Male or female?

- *Content.* Information-rich or just a jump page? Hit and run or archival? Does the content live up to the site title or blurbs? Is the text clear, well written, and well organized?

- *Appearance.* Good graphic sense? Do graphics enhance content or just decorate? Does the author make excessive use of graphics?

- *Accessibility.* Does the page load quickly? Does it require special plug-ins like Java or Shockwave?

- *Organization.* Is the site easily navigable? Does it require lots of scrolling? Are there lots of page jumps? Is there any "link rot" (links that go nowhere)? Is there any confusion about where Back or Next might lead?

Here are some general tips on reviewing Websites:

- Judge by modest standards. Not everyone has the resources or skill to produce flawless, imaginative work.

- Judge by the author's evident purpose, not by what you wish the author's purpose had been.

- Judge honestly and objectively. Identify your biases and make allowances for them.

- Discuss style (the "body language" or nonverbal message of the site).

- Ask what the work implies by its success or failure. Does it imply that the business understands how to market on the Web, or that professional Web designers still aren't very good at Web design?

If you can articulate your responses to good and bad Websites, you'll be able to do the same for your own — and others who review your site will have more kind things to say about it.

Exercise 1: Converting Prose to Bullets

Convert the following paragraph to a bulleted list. Compare your version with the one in the back of the book.

> Science fiction evolved from earlier genres and has kept some of their conventions. These include an isolated society, whether an island, a lost valley, or a distant planet; a morally significant language, such as Orwell's Newspeak; documents that play an important role in the story, like the Book of Bokonon in Vonnegut's *Cat's Cradle;* an ideological attitude toward sex, as in Huxley's *Brave New World;* and an inquisitive outsider, like Genly Ai in Le Guin's *The Left Hand of Darkness.*
>
> *[80 words]*

_____

_____

_____

_____

_____

_____

_____

_____

_____

_____

_____

_____

4
WRITING GOOD WEBTEXT

You have two main sources of material for your site: brand-new, self-created text, or text from other sources (e.g., annual reports, résumés, and technical memorandums). When you're importing text from print sources, you may have little choice: the site may simply be the archive of items that have to remain exactly as written. But in some cases, you may indeed have to adapt text from other sources to make it easily usable on the Web.

Unless you've done very little writing for print, you're going to bring all kinds of habits from the print medium to the Web. That's fine; much of what goes on your site will end up on paper anyway, and the basics of good writing are the same in any medium.

Let's consider those basics in the light of the two Information principles mentioned in Chapter 2:

- *Clarity:* Webwriting should be understandable at first glance.
- *Correctness:* Webwriting should reflect proper English usage and appropriate nonverbal messages.

To make sure that your writing is understandable at first glance, and that your writing is correct, consider the following suggestions.

When you are using text from another source, you need to be aware of copyright issues. See Chapter 9 for a discussion of copyright.

Activate the Passive

The passive voice is an occupational hazard in many fields: Science, technical specialties, academic writing, and bureaucracy are all rich sources of the passive voice. It's so common that most writers in such fields don't even know when they're using it — and if they do know, they're actually proud of themselves for doing so. They think they sound professional.

In the active voice, you always know who's doing what:

I studied the novels of Ursula K. LeGuin.

Pol Pot massacred hundreds of thousands of Cambodians.

Tim Berners-Lee invented the World Wide Web in 1989.

Most readers are very comfortable with the active voice, but in technical and bureaucratic writing, the active voice can draw attention to the writer or actor:

I tested 33 subjects for Ebola fever.

The *inspectors* found several minor infractions.

You made a serious mistake.

Technical and bureaucratic writers tend to avoid this kind of attention. They prefer to write:

Thirty-three subjects *were tested* for Ebola fever.

Several minor infractions *were found.*

A serious mistake *was made.*

This puts attention on the action, not the actors, and sometimes that's exactly what you want. It also appears more objective, because the actors disappear. At most, the actor turns up at the end of the sentence in a prepositional phrase:

Several minor infractions were found *by the inspectors.*

A serious mistake was made *by you.*

For writers who want to seem objective, and therefore more credible, the passive voice is dangerously attractive. That's because people who use passive voice a lot are likely to use it where it doesn't belong. Imagine your partner saying about your cooking: "Dinner was greatly enjoyed by me." Imagine yourself replying: "Your comments are very much appreciated." You'd both sound like stuffed shirts, and if you write your Webtext the same way, your readers will think you really are a stuffed shirt — or at best a dull and wordy writer.

Don't Confuse Passive Voice with Past Tense

If you write "I enjoyed dinner," you're using active voice and past tense. If you write "Dinner was enjoyed by me," you're still in past tense (dinner happened in the past), but you're in passive voice: The person who did the enjoying is lost in a prepositional phrase (by me) at the end of the sentence, instead of being the subject at the beginning of the sentence.

Passive voice raises another problem for Webwriters: it means more words. "I enjoyed dinner" is three words; "Dinner was enjoyed by me" is five. You are asking your poor reader to plow through two extra words for no good reason.

Sometimes, of course, you really do want to keep attention on the act, and not the actor. Maybe it's more important to mention that a mistake was made, without blaming anyone in particular. In those cases you should use passive voice — but use it consciously, when it serves your purpose, not just because you think it sounds professional.

Choose Concrete Anglo-Saxon Words

If you are conversant in English, you have the incredible luck to speak and write a language that falls in love with every other language it meets. English will borrow words from other languages all over the world, and then forget to return them.

English speakers weren't always so promiscuous. When Christianity first converted Britain, the Roman missionaries had to translate crux (cross) as rood because their converts preferred their own Germanic language. But when the French-speaking Normans conquered Britain, they imposed their Latin-based language on the country. So the French croix, from Latin crux, became the Modern English cross. French and Latin were the languages of culture and law. Words from Anglo-Saxon Old English tended to stay in the mud of the barnyard.

So we now have two main streams in English: words from the Latin (and Greek), which we use for technical, scientific, bureaucratic, and scholarly writing, and Anglo-Saxon words, which we use in everyday conversation. Greco-Latin words tend to be abstract and hard to visualize. Anglo-Saxon words are concrete and easy to visualize. When we "cause collateral damage," it's hard to understand that we are "killing unlucky bystanders." In some cases, the Latin word has largely replaced the Anglo-Saxon one and we're stuck with the Latin. If we talk about "folks in North Carolina" instead of "people in North Carolina," we're going to sound a little too casual — even if "people" is Latin and "folks" is Anglo-Saxon.

On balance, though, Anglo-Saxon words are more immediate and understandable than Greco-Latin ones. Unless you're writing for highly specialized readers on a topic with a Greco-Latin technical vocabulary, choose the Anglo-Saxon word over the Greco-Latin one. (Most good dictionaries will list the origin of a word — OE means Old English, for example, and Gk means Greek. The definition may also give a more usable synonym for a rare word.)

Use Simple Sentences

Depending on their organization, sentences can be simple, compound, complex, or compound-complex. Here are examples of each:

(a) Simple sentence: *This Website celebrates the career of Holly Cole* (subject: "Website," verb: "celebrates").

(b) Compound sentence: *This Website celebrates the career of Holly Cole, and it also provides links to other Canadian singers' sites* ("and" links to second subject, "it," and second verb, "provides").

(c) Complex sentence: *This Website celebrates the career of Holly Cole, who is a Canadian jazz singer* (simple sentence with a subordinate clause attached — "who is a Canadian jazz singer").

A subordinate clause is one that can't stand on its own; it must be part of an independent clause, which is a complete sentence.

(d) Compound-complex sentence: *This Website celebrates the career of Holly Cole, who is a Canadian jazz singer, and it also provides links to other Canadian singers' sites* (two independent clauses, linked by "and," with one independent clause modified by a subordinate clause).

You'll probably agree that the first sentence, the simple sentence, is the easiest to read. The longer a sentence becomes, the harder to read it becomes. Remember also that your readers may not have set their Web browsers to show text in a large, readable font. Short, simple sentences will be much easier for everyone to understand quickly.

This is especially true of your front page, where many readers will first arrive. If that page is a solid mass of complex text, stretching clear across the screen, many readers will simply surf on to somewhere else. If your front page is just a brief introduction to the site's topics, plus a table of contents, simple sentences (and even phrases) are all you need.

Don't feel you have to write in a dumbed-down style, though. By all means vary your sentence patterns, if only to hold reader interest. But most sentences should be short and simple.

What if you're archiving long texts written in a complex style? Fine — your readers will probably want to download them to read later, either on-screen or as printouts.

Avoid Clichés

Avoid clichés like the plague. A cliché is a phrase or expression that was once so new and surprising that everyone repeated it. Like an unspoiled tourist destination ruined by too many tourists, the cliché loses its whole reason for existence when everyone uses it.

Clichés have several forms. Proverbial clichés include the stitch in time that saves nine, too many cooks spoiling the broth, and the ounce of prevention that saves a pound of cure. Sometimes you can get away with these by letting readers know that you know you're offering a stale but (barely) usable term: "Here's the proverbial ounce of prevention that will save you a pound of cure."

Slangy clichés have the embarrassing look of someone who thinks the 1970s are still happening. When you read terms like uptight, outasight, and far out, you're dealing with someone in a time warp (if that's not a cliché too). If you're very careful you may be able to get away with dead slang if you use it ironically. "Kewl" for "cool" is an attempt to do so — though not a very successful attempt. (Scholars of slang may recall that before "cool" took over in the late 1950s, the "hepcats" described anything they really admired as "real George." That one, at least, died a merciful death.)

Trendy clichés are a little different. Slang tends to come from marginal groups like ethnic minorities; trendy clichés come from the mass media's journalists and commentators, the "chattering classes" (there's a trendy cliché in itself). People who write or speak for a living tend — to use yet another cliché — to drink each other's bathwater. One of them will come up with an unusual word or phrase, and everyone else seizes on it. Before you know it, everyone on CNN or the editorial page of your local paper is talking about interfaces, closure, and empowerment.

The media have given us some of their own occupational slang, like "sound bite," but trendy clichés usually come from the occupations and professions most interesting to the chattering classes. So business has given us bottom lines, deep pockets, and downsizing. The military has given us bite the bullet, in the trenches, breakthrough, and flak. Engineering gives us parameters, state of the art, leading edge, and reinventing the wheel. Athletics gives us team players, ballpark figures, level playing fields, and track records. Politics is the home of charisma, spin doctors, bandwagons, and momentum. The self-help movement takes us from trendy clichés to what many consider outright psychobabble: self-actualizing, holistic, meaningful, one day at a time, and wellness.

When you look at a Website, pay attention to the text. Does it resort to clichés or jargon? Of what kind? What is the effect created by the clichés or jargon? Can you imagine why the writer used them? And can you imagine how the text might read with the clichés removed?

You might try downloading text from a site and then revising it to remove all clichés. You're likely to find that your version is much stronger and more effective than the original.

Choose Strong Verbs over Weak Ones

A hazard of business writing is the tendency to take a good, strong verb and turn it into a noun or phrase — and then to put a weak verb in its place. Consider the following:

- Make a decision/Decide
- Conduct a survey of/Survey
- Make allowance for/Allow for
- Make use of/Use
- Serves to explain/Explains
- By application of pressure/By pressing
- Do a review/Review
- Perform a test/Test
- Make a comeback/Come back

The first phrases are longer, and may sound better to some people, but prefer the shorter ones unless you have some urgent reason to write longer. At least think about why the longer term would be better before you use it.

Be Aware of Dialect Variations

A dialect is a form of a language specific to a particular region that most local residents can generally understand, but which they may not use themselves. So a Scot from Edinburgh and an Australian from Melbourne will be able to converse in English, but they won't speak in the same accent or with quite the same vocabulary.

In different English dialects, the same word can mean different things. In American English, a bluff is a low cliff; in Canadian English, it means a grove of trees on the prairie. And different words can mean the same thing.

In Standard English, for example, "flaunt" means "to show off," and "flout" means "to break a rule in public." Most North Americans, however, will talk about someone "flaunting the law," but they don't mean waving the constitution around — they mean publicly breaking the law. In their dialects, that's what "flaunt" means. This may be incorrect Standard English, but it's perfectly understandable even to Standard English speakers. The problem is that non-Standard usage may distract readers from the message. (In fairness, speakers and writers of Standard English may seem stuffy or pedantic to others; but Standard remains the most widely understandable and accepted dialect.)

If you intend your Website strictly for people who speak your own dialect, or you're trying for a strong local flavor, you can ignore Standard English. If you're trying to reach a broad audience, however, Standard English is your best choice. If you're unsure about what's considered Standard, countless manuals on English usage are available. Look in your library's reference section or a large local bookstore. Many dictionaries also include sections on grammar, spelling, and punctuation.

Be Precise

You may also mislead your readers by choosing a word that's not quite what you mean. Suppose you're writing text for the Chesterton Website and you decide to put in a link to current weather reports and forecasts. Do you call it Chesterton Climate Report or Chesterton Weather Report? Well, "climate" refers to weather conditions over a period of months or years; "weather" refers to what's going on at the moment. Chesterton may have a dry climate, but it may also be expecting a downpour tonight. Be sure to choose your words precisely.

Diction: Choose Your Words Carefully

Diction refers to the choice of words used to express an idea. Here are some words that may cause confusion if you choose them for the wrong purpose. Sometimes they sound like the term you want, or they've been misused so constantly that they sound right to you.

- *Adverse:* harmful, negative. Some antibiotics cause adverse reactions in patients.

- *Averse:* reluctant, opposed. She was averse to confronting her boss about the problem.

- *Affect* (verb): to influence. This news will badly affect our share prices.

- *Effect* (noun): result. This news had a bad effect on our share prices.

- *Aggravate:* make worse. This news will only aggravate our image in the market.

- *Irritate:* annoy. The board members were irritated by the bad news.

- *Alot:* incorrect form of "a lot." A lot of people make this mistake.

- *Allot:* to divide or apportion. We can allot 50 seats on a first-come basis.

- *Allude to:* suggest without naming. He alluded to his earlier successes.

- *Refer to:* name directly. She referred to her best-selling Harry Potter books.

- *Alright:* incorrect form of All right.

- *Ambiguous:* having two or more meanings. "Biweekly" is ambiguous because it could mean twice a week or once every two weeks.

- *Ambivalent:* having mixed or conflicting feelings. I feel ambivalent about challenging him on this issue.

- *Among:* refers to three or more. The prize money was divided among the four winners.

- *Between:* refers to two. The prize money was divided between the two winners.

- *Amount:* refers to uncountable singular items. Feeding an army requires a large amount of flour.

- *Number:* refers to plural items. Feeding an army requires a large number of trained cooks.

- *Apparently:* presumably, by appearances. Since he didn't answer the door, he's apparently left the house.

- *Obviously:* without doubt, plainly. Since we've searched the house, he's obviously left.

- *Assume:* accept as a premise in an argument. Let's assume we bring in a flat tax.

- *Presume:* take for granted. I presume his government will bring in a flat tax.

- *Assure:* to promise. We can assure you of a great stay in our B&B.

- *Ensure:* to make certain. You can ensure success by careful planning.

- *Insure:* to guarantee against loss. Here's how to insure all your valuables with one policy.

- *Canvas:* coarse cloth. The canvas sails were in shreds.

- *Canvass:* to seek support. She will canvass the delegates on behalf of her candidate.

- *Cement:* component of concrete; binding agent. Let's cement our agreement with a toast!

- *Concrete:* hard material used for construction. The concrete overpass collapsed without warning.

- *Censor:* to delete or suppress sensitive or dangerous information. The government censored reports from the battlefield.

- *Censure:* to condemn or disapprove. The protestors censured the government's suppression of the news.

- *Cite:* quote or summon. I can cite several authorities. They were cited for speeding.

- *Sight:* to see or take aim. Dave Johnson sighted a UFO on April 2.

- *Site:* location. This is a good site for links to Malaysian businesses.

- *Client:* user of the services of a business or of a non-medical professional. As a client of Textor, you can expect the best in Web design.

- *Customer:* person who buys from a store or business. As a customer of Self-Counsel Press, you're assured of prompt deliveries.

- *Climax:* highest point, turning point in a story. The book's climax is deeply shocking.

- *Crescendo:* growing in loudness or intensity. The crescendo of applause ended with a standing ovation.

- *Complement:* to complete, or a total. This tie will complement your suit very well. The ship carries a complement of 32 crew members.

- *Compliment:* to praise. I must compliment you on that elegant tie.

- *Compose:* make or create. This committee is composed of six industry representatives.

- *Comprise:* include or embrace. This committee comprises six industry representatives. (Note: Never say "comprised of.")

- *Convince:* to win an argument through appeals to logic and intellect. The experiment convinced even the skeptics.

- *Persuade:* to win an argument through appeals to emotion. His tears and choked voice persuaded her of his sincerity.

- *Country:* the territory of a nation. Canada is a very large country.

- *Nation:* the people of a country. Canadians are a largely peaceable nation.

- *Dependant:* a person who relies on another. My daughters are my dependants.

- *Dependent:* variable, depending on. Our starting time will be dependent on the weather.

- *Desert:* desolate, to abandon, or something deserved. The rocky desert stretched to the horizon. He deserted his companions. The king praised each knight according to his desert.

- *Dessert:* a sweet. We had key lime pie for dessert.

- *Different from:* used before a noun or pronoun. Taxco is different from Cuernavaca.

- *Different than:* used before a clause. Taxco was different than I had expected.
- *Disc:* correct spelling for all non-computer references: A compact disc, a herniated disc.
- *Disk:* correct spelling for computer references: a ZIP disk, a floppy disk.
- *Disinterested:* impartial, neutral. A disinterested arbitrator resolved the dispute.
- *Uninterested:* not interested. The arbitrator was uninterested in minor issues.
- *Effective:* having a desired result; coming into operation. The new policy, effective on Monday, should be an improvement.
- *Effectual:* performing as desired. Her arguments were effectual in winning the debate.
- *Every day:* each day. We record the air temperature four times every day.
- *Everyday:* routine. Recording air temperature is an everyday activity for us.
- *Fewer:* used with countable plural items. We've had fewer hits on our site this month than last month.
- *Less:* used with uncountable singular items. We have less traffic on our site this month than last month.
- *Gibe:* insult, mock. I'm tired of your asinine gibes.
- *Jibe:* fit, agree. Your estimate jibes with ours.
- *Healthful:* promoting good health. Vegetables form part of a healthful diet.
- *Healthy:* in good health. She remained healthy and alert well into her 90s.
- *Hoard:* a supply of something. We have a hoard of canned goods in the basement.
- *Horde:* a large number of people. A horde of bargain-hunters swarmed into the shop.

- *Home in on:* approach a desired goal. The pilot homed in on the radio beacon's signal.

- *Hone in on:* incorrect but widespread usage; "hone" means "sharpen," so the expression is meaningless.

- *Imply:* suggest, hint. I don't mean to imply that the mistake was deliberate.

- *Infer:* conclude, deduce. From the evidence, we can infer that the mistake was accidental.

- *Incidence:* rate of occurrence. The incidence of drug-resistant tuberculosis is growing rapidly.

- *Incident:* event. We've all learned from this unfortunate incident.

- *Irregardless:* incorrect or humorous corruption of "regardless."

- *Its:* belonging to it. The committee has a lot on its agenda.

- *It's:* contraction of "it is" or "it has." It's going to be a long meeting. It's been raining all afternoon. (By the way, its' is not a word at all.)

- *Loath:* reluctant, averse. He was loath to confront the problem.

- *Loathe:* detest, hate. He loathes his adversaries.

- *Moral:* having to do with good and evil. We faced a painful moral decision.

- *Morale:* group spirit. Morale in the office sank when we heard the news.

- *Perquisite:* a special privilege (perk). A new car is one of the perquisites of the job.

- *Prerequisite:* a condition or requirement. A BA is a pre-requisite for admission to our program.

- *Principal:* first or most important. My principal motive was to create a simple, elegant Website.

- *Principle:* rule or idea. We support the principle of free speech on the Web.

- *Proponent:* advocate. She is a proponent of free speech on the Web.

- *Protagonist:* central character in a story. Ged is the protagonist of Ursula K. Le Guin's Earthsea novels.

- *Reign:* time of a monarch's rule. England prospered during the reign of Elizabeth I.

- *Rein:* harness or control. Our teacher kept us on a tight rein.

- *Seasonable:* appropriate to the season. Rainfall has been seasonable this summer.

- *Seasonal:* pertaining to the season. We've broken the seasonal record for rain this summer.

- *Toe the line:* conform. The soldiers formed even ranks by toeing the line.

- *Tow the line:* incorrect usage, a misspelling of "toe the line."

- *Waive:* give up. You can waive your right to a jury trial.

- *Wave:* move back and forth. Wave good-bye to your hard-won rights!

- *Weaved:* past tense of weave meaning to avoid hitting something, or to contrive an involved story. The striker weaved through the defenders on his way to the goal. He weaved an incredible tale of adventure and derring-do.

- *Wove:* past tense of weave meaning a fabric. Penelope wove endlessly at her loom.

You will have noticed that, in many of these cases, the difference between using the correct term and the incorrect one can be a spelling error that the spell checker on your computer will miss. That's also true of many other words: to, two, and too; there, their, and they're; coarse and course. Chances are you already know the words you have trouble with, so check them repeatedly against a dictionary until you're sure you're using them correctly.

Don't Use Extended Metaphors

In print text we may develop an argument through contrast and comparison — that is, by showing how two things are different or similar. Again we use transition words and phrases:

Unlike the dungeons, the castle's main floor is well furnished.

Just as in Cuernavaca, your hosts in Taxco will make you feel very welcome.

In hypertext, as Robert E. Horn advises in his book *Mapping Hypertext,* we can use such contrasts and comparisons only within a single section. The same is true of extended metaphors. In a print document, you might describe a government as a "ship of state," with the executive as the bridge, the legislature as the engine room, and so on. This extended metaphor may work to help unify a passage of many paragraphs. But in hypertext, with readers skipping around in no predictable order, their first encounter with such a metaphor may be baffling.

Use Clear Antecedents

Hypertext must always include the antecedent for every pronoun in a given section. If I write "She went on to earn a PhD in physics at MIT," I'd better mention her name earlier in the same section; otherwise readers won't know who "she" is.

Grammar and Usage: Common Errors

Whether you're in New Zealand or New York, chances are you make the same errors in Standard English. Here are some of the most common errors:

Sentence fragments

Your sentence will be a fragment if it lacks a subject or a verb. Here are some examples of fragments and their corrected versions:

- Which surprised everyone./This surprised everyone.

- Really weird./I think that's really weird.

- A superb musician but a troubled human being./She was a superb musician but a troubled human being.

- Not bloody likely!/That's not bloody likely!

Sentence fragments are often fine in captions and blurbs, where the reader doesn't really need a full sentence. So a tag like "Joe Doakes in happier days" under a photo of Joe is all your readers require. A button linking to photos of your wedding can read "The Big Day!" instead of "Come This Way to See Photos of Our Wedding Day."

However, in text where you're trying to explain or describe something in detail, avoid sentence fragments.

Subject-verb disagreements

Subject-verb disagreements are easy errors to make if you forget which word is your subject. For example:

> The leader of the frightened soldiers were unable to make them cease firing.

Because "soldiers" is close to the verb, many people might make the verb plural (were) to agree with it. But look again — it was the soldiers' leader, not the soldiers themselves, who couldn't make them stop firing. The correct verb should be singular (was).

In other cases we have a compound subject but we mistakenly treat the two nouns like a single unit:

> Snow and sleet makes hiking dangerous on these trails.

> Spelling and grammar is my big problem in English.

In some cases, however, we really can treat a plural as a singular:

> Six months is the standard probationary period.

> A million dollars is still a lot of money.

> Richards and Johnson is a distinguished legal firm.

And just to make things really confusing, sometimes we can describe a single thing or person with more than one noun and we still use a singular verb:

The lawyer and human-rights activist has enjoyed great success. (One person with two titles.)

The singer and songwriter has won a Grammy. (One person with two skills.)

If you're worried about subject-verb errors and you're not sure which noun is the subject, ask yourself: Who or what is performing the action of the verb in this sentence? Who's enjoyed success? Who's won two Grammies? The answer is your subject.

Incorrect pronouns

We use pronouns to stand in for nouns when repeating the nouns would sound awkward:

Dora released her latest video last month, and she says she's happy with it.

Imagine using "Dora" four times in that sentence:

Dora released Dora's latest video last month, and Dora says Dora's happy with it.

We sometimes run into trouble when we forget that some pronouns are subjective (that is, they perform the action of the verb in the sentence) and others are objective (they receive the action of the verb).

He emailed her. She emailed him.

We'd laugh if we read:

Her emailed he. Him likes she a lot.

But many people, in conversation and in writing, will say:

She emailed him and I.

Me and her went to the conference.

Her and her husband set up a home-based business.

Evidently they think that the rules don't apply if they're talking about more than one person! But the rules do apply:

> She emailed him and me.
>
> She and I went to the conference.
>
> She and her husband set up a home-based business.

Another pronoun problem is "myself," which some people use incorrectly. Pronouns with "self" are either reflexive or emphatic:

> I asked myself a question (action of verb turns back on the asker).
>
> I myself told you it wouldn't work (emphasizes who told you).

Don't use "myself" as a long-winded way to say "I" or "me":

> Joan and myself went to the conference.
>
> My wife and myself set up a home-based business.

Misuse of adjective for adverb

Adjectives modify nouns: a good man, a fast computer. Adverbs modify verbs, adjectives, and other adverbs: a truly good man, a really fast computer. Sometimes you can change the meaning of a sentence by using (or misusing) some common adjectives: "You did good by winning the contest" is incorrect, but "You did good by raising flood-relief money" is correct. We do well when we perform with style and excellence. We do good when we make the world a better place.

These are just four common grammar and usage problem areas. For details on these and many other hazards of usage, spelling, and punctuation, consult almost any composition handbook or dictionary.

Exercise 2: Activating the Passive

Revise these sentences to activate the passive voice and then check your answers against those in the back of the book.

1. It is argued by some researchers that alien bodies were retrieved by the US Air Force from a crashed spacecraft near Roswell, New Mexico, in 1947.

    _____

    _____

    _____

2. Miles Davis's "Sketches of Spain" was hailed by critics as one of his finest works.

    _____

    _____

    _____

3. The graphic user interface was originally developed by researchers at Xerox.

    _____

    _____

    _____

4. A cholera outbreak in 19th-century London was stopped when a neighborhood water pump's handle was removed by a local physician.

    _____

    _____

    _____

Exercise 2 — continued

5. These graphics have been chosen carefully to illustrate each step of the process.

_____

_____

Exercise 3: Using Anglo-Saxon Vocabulary

Replace each of the following words with an Anglo-Saxon word or phrase (or a more common Greco-Latin word):

1. Altercation _____

2. Antagonist _____

3. Capitulate _____

4. Celestial _____

5. Demotic _____

6. Epitome _____

7. Fiduciary _____

8. Gravamen _____

9. Impediment _____

10. Litigious _____

If you can't find a shorter, clearer word without checking your dictionary, imagine how your readers would feel if they didn't have a dictionary at all. Now that you know these words, do your readers a favor: don't use them in your Webtext!

5
EDITING WEBTEXT

In ancient Rome, the title of the person who sponsored a gladiatorial fight to the death was Editor. Maybe because of that association with hacking and slashing, modern writers are often suspicious of editors. They shouldn't be. A good editor can save you from countless embarrassing mistakes while helping you make your points more coherently, more eloquently, and even more gracefully.

What's more, you can be your own editor. Here are some steps you can take to improve your own text once you've drafted it.

Trash Your Spell Checker

Computer spell checkers are rubber crutches: they fail just when you need them most. All they do is compare what you've written with a list of words, and if they find the word in their list, they say it's okay. So you may have written "their" when you meant to write "there," or "your" when you meant "you're," and the spell checker will tell you it's correct.

The spell checker will of course catch outright typos, doubled words, and other errors, so it has some usefulness in that regard. But a quick skim of your document, flagging obvious goofs, is the best you can hope for from a spell checker.

If you have a grammar and style checker, you're a little better off, but not much. Style checkers can spot bad habits like overuse of the passive voice, or too many prepositional phrases. This at least forces you to think about whether you have to indulge in such habits.

Your style checker can also give you a sense of the reading level of your text. It does so by counting the number of syllables per word, the number of words per sentence, and the number of sentences per 100 words. The fewer the syllables, the fewer the number of words per sentence, and the more sentences per 100 words, the lower your reading level — usually expressed as a grade level. (This book is readable at the grade 7 level, for example.)

If your site is aimed at a general audience, especially one including young children or persons who don't read English fluently, it's common sense to keep the reading level as low as the subject permits. You don't get extra points for making your text readable only to PhD candidates. Clearly you don't want to dumb down your text needlessly, but a lower reading level makes your text understandable to more people. And the point of a Website, after all, is to make information available to as many people as possible.

Cut Verbiage

Your hit and run text is all that most of your readers will bother with. Only the really dedicated people will actually look at your archived text and perhaps download it for careful reading. Therefore your hit and run text should be as brief as possible, so it delivers its message clearly and quickly.

If you set yourself an arbitrary word limit — for example, no chunk of text may run over 75 words — you will be amazed at how easy it is to cut the fat out of your text. I suggest as a first step that you deliberately write long chunks of text: maybe 150 or 200 words. Then start cutting words until you're down to 55 or 60 words; now you have the luxury of actually adding some words. Every sentence, every phrase, every word has had to fight for its life. Nothing is there just because it sounds good — you're writing, remember, not making music! You've packed the maximum meaning into the minimum text, so your readers will get the message in the shortest possible time.

Critique Your Own Text

A writer lives inside your head, and so does an editor. They don't always get along. The writer is having a great time being creative and showing off his vocabulary; the editor is watching over the writer's shoulder and tearing her hair out. While the writer is cranking out Great Prose, the editor is screaming herself hoarse about what drivel this all is. The writer doesn't hear the details, but starts feeling nervous. "Maybe this isn't all that good after all," he mutters. Finally he decides something's gone horribly wrong (heaven knows what), and he abandons the job.

Sound familiar?

It doesn't have to be that way. If you were a best-selling author, you could send your messed-up manuscript to your high-priced editor, who would tell you exactly what was going right and wrong with the manuscript and offer detailed advice on improvements. What if you don't have the services of a professional editor? Well, you have an editor living right inside your skull — all you have to do is give her a chance to put her criticisms into words.

So as you're putting your Webtext together, keep a diary or journal in which you can make notes to yourself about how your writing is going. If a problem does arise, your inner editor can sound off about it ("The introduction is way too long and too cute, and you don't need to use the word 'fiduciary'").

Once you've put the problem into words, something startling happens: The solution follows almost instantly. When you start organizing your ideas into sentences and paragraphs, the process seems to free the creative part of your mind, and it comes up with answers that you'd never get if you just pounded your head against the edge of your desk. Sometimes the answer comes before you've finished writing the sentence describing the problem.

Self-critiques don't just help with problems of style. Your inner editor may also warn you about problems in the organization of your whole site. Maybe you want to list a bunch of excellent links to other sites on your front page; your editor, if you give her the chance, will tell you not to be an idiot: "Put them down in the basement so readers don't find them until they've looked at all your own stuff."

Print out to Proofread

You simply cannot trust your own proofreading abilities unless you proofread from paper. Not only is computer-screen text hard to read, it's hard to proofread as well. That means real trouble for you as a Webwriter: Your text may look subliterate even if only mistyped, but it will be very hard for you to catch your typos if you're proofreading only on the screen. The longer you try, the less accurate you'll be because monitor reading will tire you out. Your readers, however, will come to your site fresh and unfamiliar with your text. So they'll spot those typos every time.

Sections that you haven't changed much are especially dangerous. On my first Website, I didn't look at my headline after I'd written it; when I installed the site, the headline featured an embarrassing typo — which I didn't catch until after I'd invited dozens of colleagues to take a look.

When you print out your site to proofread it, don't print out your text in 10-point single-spaced text. Make it 14-point and double spaced, use an unfamiliar font, and let it sit overnight before you proofread. That way your text will look unfamiliar. You'll have to read what's actually on the paper, not what's on the inside of your forehead — and errors are more likely to leap out at you.

Here's another useful tip: Read your text out loud. That will also force you to read every word, instead of just skimming. You may find some awkward phrases that looked okay on the screen and on paper, but that sound clumsy or suggest an unintended meaning. Better to catch them now.

Does this sound like a lot of hassle for a humble little Web page about your favorite singer or your dog-walking service? Maybe so, but typos, bad grammar, and other mechanical errors can really hurt the impact of your page. Maybe you can create amazing sounds and graphics, but if you can't spell, your readers will notice — and they won't like it. This is especially true when you have a business site promoting either your own skills or the virtues of the company that's hired you to write content for its site. Simple proofreading mistakes instantly make you look bush-league and unprofessional.

Don't Respect the Text

Maybe it's an ingrained respect for the written word going back to ancient Babylon when only the sacred priests were literate. Maybe it just goes back to the days of the manual typewriter, when a minor error or afterthought meant re-typing the whole page.

Whatever the reason, we revere text too much. It gives us a deadly dangerous readiness to dump print-for-paper onto a Website and think we've done our job.

Respect for text is bad enough for print-media writers; on the Web, it's disastrous. In print, we expect readers to skip right along from point to point. If our text is wordy or complex, we rely on readers to get the point pretty quickly anyway. Maybe we even tell ourselves that our ideas are so subtle and nuanced that only an elaborate style will convey them adequately.

On the Web, readers need only hit the "back" button to dismiss our illusions. If we want to attract them, hold them, and inspire them to react to what we've said, we need to look at our text with a cold, dispassionate eye.

Jakob Nielsen tells us the computer monitor slows down reading speed by up to 25 percent, but we haven't yet accepted the implication: that everything we adapt from print to Web should be at least 25 percent shorter. Print-media text assumes readers will sit still for a long, interwoven argument; when Web surfers find such arguments, too often they just surf on to somewhere else. And when that happens we've squandered the great advantage the Web gives us as writers: the chance to engage our readers in dialogue.

Some print materials, of course, don't need adaptation because they're simply archived on the site. An annual report, a survey, an article once published in a newspaper — these can remain at full length. As pdf (portable document format) files, they can even retain their original formatting.

But for Web users who are simply scanning your site, you should try to provide a kind of smorgasbord, with everything available at a glance. To make scanning easier, you need to adapt most print texts by including:

- Self-explanatory titles on your contents pages, so scanners will know what they're heading for when they click through.

- Blurbs, in case the titles really aren't all that self-explanatory.

- Headings that either form titles for individual chunks of text, or divide even a single screenful of text into two or three segments.

- "Condensed" text that conveys the key elements as concisely as possible — perhaps with links to the original-length archived item for those who want every detail.

The condensation process demands the most disrespect for print-source text. A useful guideline is to cut such text by not just 25 percent, but 50 percent, just to see if it's possible. If the result can't stand on its own, then restore some of the original text (or a concise version of it) until a scanner, arriving directly on this chunk, will understand what it's about.

And not only understand it — respond to it! Maybe you want your readers to respond by jumping to the archived original, or emailing your organization, or buying the product. Whatever the response desired, the text should make it an easy, attractive choice. What's more, the choice itself should spark a positive response from the Website:

> Congratulations! Your first email newsletter is on its way! Let us know what you think of it.

> Thank you for your purchase. It should reach you within 48 hours. Meanwhile, your user manual is already in your mailbox.

Maybe you feel awkward about disrespecting the text, but what's really important is that you give utmost respect to the visitors who have honored you with their presence on your site. Whatever you can do to make their visit interesting, surprising, and successful — including presenting text as clearly and concisely as possible — should make it clear that their needs come first.

Edit for International Readers

When you write for the Web, remember that it really is worldwide. Most readers may be native English speakers, but many are not. Soon a majority of Web users will not be native English speakers, and even native speakers may have trouble with particular dialects. For example, a "car smash" in Memphis is a "fender bender" in California. When an Australian man has a "mate," it's his male friend and not his wife.

If we're going to meet the needs of our worldwide readers, we have to make our language as simple and clear as possible. This isn't easy. A Brazilian journalist is translating this book, and I stumped him (what is "stumped"?) right in the title of Chapter 1, "Hype and Hypertext." What, he wanted to know, is "hype"? It wasn't in his English-Portuguese dictionary. Recently I asked a Chinese penpal for her snailmail address; she sent me her Hotmail address instead... because she thought "snailmail" must mean an email account that opens very slowly.

Does this mean that we have to set our grammar checkers to flag anything that might make a third-grader frown? Do we have to define every word?

No — at least, not usually. The other day I referred a foreign student to my college's Website for advice about admissions and fees. The information for foreign students wasn't written very simply. After all, if its readers can't understand routine college-level English, they're not yet ready for us.

Similarly, foreign professionals may be very much at ease with the technical English of their profession, even if their colloquial English is awkward. So a technical site need not oversimplify its content.

In some cases, you may even want to emphasize your dialect to remind readers that they're not in Kansas anymore. A Canadian site can offer an exotic flavour to American visitors if its writers labour to spell British-style. It can also use distinctly Canadian terms, like "saltchuck" for "salt water" and "bluff" for "grove of trees." If your site's dialect is likely to baffle too many visitors, a glossary may help.

Many readers will grasp unfamiliar terms just from context, but the context can be blunt or subtle: "We went out on the saltchuck, which is what some British Columbians call salt water." Or: "We went out on the saltchuck, braving choppy waves in our sea kayaks."

So for technical sites, or "exotic" sites, specialized dialects will be fine. A site designed for general readers, however, should probably stick to bare-bones Standard English — a vocabulary of widely understood words with very few regional, slangy, or idiomatic expressions.

Am I being a terrible spoilsport who disapproves of having fun with English? I should hope not! As George Orwell said in the last of his rules for clear English: "Break any of these rules sooner than say something outright barbarous."

And don't forget one priceless advantage you have as a Webwriter — you can encourage and provoke your readers to ask questions about the unusual words and phrases on your site. Your content isn't just a take-it-or-leave-it box lunch, but a constantly changing buffet of interesting and sometimes mysterious items. If customers find you eager to explain what's on offer, they'll be delighted to learn and experiment — and you'll learn how much you still have to learn about your own language.

A Webwriter's Style Guide

Creating Your Own Style Guide
Your organization may well need its own in-house style guide to ensure correctness and consistency with practice in your business or profession. I strongly recommend Renee Hopkins's excellent, step-by-step advice at "Edit-works" where she shows just how to put a style guide together: <http://www.edit-work.com/>

Journalists and academics use style guides. So do book and magazine editors. They're writing for print on paper, in genres that are centuries old. The Web has existed for less than a decade; would a generally accepted Webstyle guide be a premature straitjacket, or an overdue step toward law and order on a wild frontier?

Well, several Webstyle guides already exist, though they're more honored in the breach than the observance. Tim Berners-Lee, the father of the Web, created such a style guide. So did Gareth Rees (though I believe his guide is now available only as an appendix in this book), and Jutta Degener's list of "dangerous words" is still controversial.

In the print media, style guides don't interest rank amateurs or literary geniuses. Amateurs don't know the rules; geniuses break them. But for professional writers, style guides are as necessary as tape measures and plumb bobs are for carpenters.

With millions of pages up on the Web now, it really helps when Websites imitate one another, as Jakob Nielsen suggested recently. New visitors don't have to spend time learning the quirks of each particular site, including language quirks.

Many Webstyle guides can therefore be descriptive, telling their readers "This is the way most people say it." That's especially true for sites catering to specialized audiences with their own dialect or technical shoptalk.

But other style guides should be prescriptive, laying down the law on everything from abbreviations to precise word usages. Newspapers and publishers use such guides for the sake of consistency, and to save their writers and editors from repeatedly researching every obscure question. I can recommend several for North American Webwriters:

USA:

The Chicago Manual of Style (14th edition). University of Chicago Press, 1993

The Associated Press Stylebook and Libel Manual. Norm Goldstein, ed. Perseus Press, 1998.

The Microsoft Manual of Style for Technical Publications (2nd edition). Microsoft Press, 1998

Canada:

CP Stylebook: A Guide for Writers and Editors, ed. Peter Buckley. Canadian Press, 1995.

The Canadian Style: A Guide to Writing and Editing. Dundurn Press, 1997.

Editing Canadian English, 2nd edition. Macfarlane Walter & Ross, 2000.

Do guides simply impose print standards where they don't belong? Such guides set limits to expression in a medium that — in theory — requires no such limits at all. Some might even argue that style guides force newcomers to adopt the vocabulary and tone of the Web's privileged early adopters.

I doubt it. Mavericks are still free to ignore (or attack) "correct" style in their preferred Web genres. But for the vast majority of users, consistent style within Web genres is as critical as consistent navigation.

What follows is a brief guide mixing both descriptive and prescriptive, with a strong emphasis on Web-related expressions and terms that may be useful for both native English speakers and those for whom English is a foreign language. Some usages are standard whether in print or in Webtext, and ignoring such usage will only distract or confuse your readers. Web jargon and slang can be especially baffling to newcomers, whether English is their native language or not. In other cases, an expression that seems vivid and fresh to you may be baffling or boring to others. In such cases, you should at least think carefully before using them.

Abbreviations

We use short forms of many words and phrases. Some are true abbreviations, while others are acronyms or initialisms. "CA" and "Calif." are both abbreviations of "California." "UNESCO" (United Nations Educational, Scientific, and Cultural Organization) is an acronym; we pronounce it as a word. Sometimes acronyms become acceptable as words themselves, like scuba (self-containing underwater breathing apparatus) and radar (radio detection and ranging). "FBI" (Federal Bureau of Investigation) and "RCMP" (Royal Canadian Mounted Police) are initialisms; we sound out each letter.

Some abbreviations may be so common that they need no explanation: UN, NATO, TNT. Even then, if you expect numerous international readers unfamiliar with English abbreviations, an explanation somewhere in your text may be helpful. If you feel you must use an abbreviation that your readers may not recognize, write out the whole term first before beginning to use the abbreviation:

He joined the National Research Council (NRC) in 1986.

In some cases, the abbreviation may need more than just a spelling-out. TNT stands for trinitrotoluene; better to say "TNT, a powerful explosive." This is especially true for abbreviations from other languages: "Pemex, Mexico's national oil corporation."

Acronyms formed only from the initial letters should be all capitals: North Atlantic Treaty Organization = NATO. (However, some British practice allows Nato.) Acronyms formed from initials and other letters in a proper name take capitals and lower case letters: National Biscuit Company = Nabisco. Acronyms formed from phrases don't take capitals: microwave amplification by stimulated emission of radiation = maser, radio detection and ranging = radar.

Unless a Greek or Latin abbreviation is universally used, prefer the English equivalent. Your reader will understand "that is" and "for example" much faster than "i.e." and "e.g."

Here are some common abbreviations, together with their complete forms and their meanings. In many cases, when such abbreviations appear in text intended for a Website, your readers will thank you if you translate them into plain English.

Business abbreviations

acct or a/c	account
AG	Allgemeine Gesellschaft, general company Aktiengesellschaft, joint stock company (German)
ARM	adjustable rate mortgage
ASAP	as soon as possible
assn./assoc.	association
ATM	automatic teller machine
atty.	attorney
bal.	balance
Bcc.	blind carbon copy
b.l., b/l, B/L	bill of lading
CEO	chief executive officer
CFO	chief financial officer
CIO	chief information officer
c/o	care of
CPS	certified professional secretary
ctn.	carton
CY	calendar year
cc, Cc	carbon copy
Cia.	compañía, company (Spanish)
Cie.	compagnie, company (French)
co., Co.	company
c.o.d.	cash (paid) on delivery
CPA	certified public accountant

dba	doing business as
dis.	discount
dtd.	dated
ea.	each
EEO	equal employment opportunity
EOM	end of month
Ext., ext.	telephone extension (for example, Ext. 337)
FAX, fax	facsimile copy
FOB, f.o.b.	free on board (delivered without charge to buyer)
frt.	freight
fwd.	forward
FY	fiscal year
FYI	for your information
GATS	General Agreement on Trade in Services
GATT	General Agreement on Tariffs and Trade
GDP	gross domestic product
G.M.	general manager
GmbH	Gesellschaft mit beschrankte Haftung (German for limited liability company)
GNP	gross national product
hdlg.	handling
HR	human resources
HRD	human resources department
ID	identification
inc., Inc.	incorporated
inst.	instant (the present month)
IOU	I owe you
LCL	less than a carload lot
LLC	limited liability company

Ltd.	Limited (stockholders' liability limited to size of their investment)
Ltée	Limitée (French for limited liability)
max.	maximum
mdse.	merchandise
mfr.	manufacturer
min.	minimum
MIS	management information systems
misc.	miscellaneous
mo.	month
NAFTA	North American Free Trade Agreement
pd.	paid
PLC, plc	public limited company (British equivalent of US corporation)
Pty	proprietary
qty.	quantity
R&D	research and development
RE, Re, re	regarding, concerning
recd., rec'd	received
rept.	report or receipt
RSVP	please reply
S.A.	sociedad anónima/société anonyme (Spanish & French for anonymous society, like limited liability)
SOP	standard operating procedure
Spa, SpA	Società per Azione (Italian for corporation)
Srl	Società a responsabilità limitata (Italian for limited responsibility, like limited liability)
treas.	treasurer
VP	vice-president
whsle.	wholesale

Business Symbols
(used in correspondence and tables)

@	at (for example, 6 copies @ $25.95 each)
&	and (usually used only in company names)
%	percent (out of 100)
$	dollar(s)
¢	cent(s)
£	British pound
¥	Japanese yen
°	degree(s) (temperature or angle)
=	is equal to
≠	is not equal to
#	number (before a numeral — #10)
#	weight in pounds (after a numeral — 10#)
'	feet (6' tall)
"	inches (6'2" tall)
"	ditto (exactly equal; the same)
¶	paragraph
§	section
x	by (11"x14"); multiplied by (3x5)

Email abbreviations

By definition these are more likely to turn up in email than on Websites, but you should be familiar with some of these abbreviations if only because they may turn up in the email that your site inspires.

AFAIK	as far as I know
BBIAB	be back in a bit
BFD	big XXX deal
BRB	be right back

BTW	by the way
FAQ	frequently asked questions
FWIW	for what it's worth
FYI	for your information
G, <G>	grin (placed after a joke or a remark intended as such)
GD&R	grinning, ducking, and running (after a humorously intended insult)
GD&R,vvf	grinning, ducking, and running, very very fast
IANAL	I am not a lawyer (but...)
IIRC	if I recall correctly
IMNSHO	in my not so humble opinion
IMO	in my opinion
IMHO	in my humble opinion
IOW	in other words
LMAO	laughing my ass off
LOL	laughing out loud
OIC	oh, I see
OTOH	on the other hand
PITA	pain in the ass
ROTFL	rolling on the floor laughing
RTFM	read the XXX manual
SYSOP	system operator (manager of a bulletin board or online forum)
TIA	thanks in advance
TIC	tongue in cheek
TTFN	ta-ta for now
TTYL	talk to you later
VBG, <VBG>	very big grin
WRT	with regard to

WYSIWYG	what you see is what you get
YMMV	your mileage may vary

Greek and Latin

A.D.	*Anno Domini*	Year of our Lord
a.m., A.M.	*ante meridiem*	before noon
anon.	*anonymous*	nameless
c. or ca.	*circa*	about (a date)
cf.	*confer*	compare
e.g.	*exempli gratia*	for example
et al.	*et alii*	and other persons
etc.	*et cetera*	and others, and so on
et seq.	*et sequens*	and the following
fl.	*floruit*	flourished
ib., ibid.	*ibidem*	in the same place
i.e.	*id est*	that is
lb.	*libra*	pound
loc. cit.	*loco citato*	in the place cited
n.b.	*nota bene*	note well
ob.	*obiit*	died
op.	*opus*	work
op. cit.	*opere citato*	in the work cited
PhD	*Philosophiae Doctor*	Doctor of Philosophy
p.m., P.M.	*post meridiem*	afternoon
pro tem	*pro tempore*	temporarily
P.S.	*post scriptum*	written afterward
pseud.	*pseudonym*	false name

Q.E.D.	*quod erat demonstrandum*	which was to be demonstrated
q.v.	*quod vide*	which see
R.I.P.	*requiescat in pace*	rest in peace
v.	*vide*	see
viz.	*videlicet*	namely
v., vs.	*versus*	against

Scholarly/general abbreviations

Note that most lowercase and "mixed" abbreviations take periods. Mixed abbreviations that begin and end with a capital letter don't take periods.

AA	associate in arts (two-year degree)
AS	associate in science (two-year degree)
BA, AB	bachelor of arts
BBA	bachelor of business administration
B.Comm.	bachelor of commerce
BS, B.Sc.	bachelor of sciences
bbl.	barrel(s)
BTU	British Thermal Unit (heat required to raise temperature of 1 pound of water by 1 degree Fahrenheit)
C.	Celsius, Centigrade
c., ©	copyright
DA	doctor of arts
DBA	doctor of business administration
DD	doctor of divinity
DDS	doctor of dental surgery/dental science
cwt.	hundredweight (100 pounds)
deg.	degree, degrees

doz.	dozen
ed.	editor, edited
EdD	doctor of education
est.	estimated
f., ff.	and the following (pages)
hp	horsepower
JD	doctor of jurisprudence
JM	master of jurisprudence
Jr.	junior (the son of someone with the same name)
JSD	doctor of the science of laws
ll.	lines
LLB	bachelor of laws
MA	master of arts
MBA	master of business administration
MD	doctor of medicine
MS, M.Sc.	master of science
MS, ms., mss.	manuscript(s)
n.d.	no date given
NGO	non-governmental organization
No., no.	numero (number)
n.p.	no numbered pages
obs.	obsolete
p., pp.	page(s)
P.Eng.	professional engineer
quango	quasi-autonomous non-governmental organization
SJ	Society of Jesus

ThD	doctor of theology
vol.	volume

Web abbreviations

For detailed definitions, consult the following Websites:

- Webopedia: <http://www.webopedia.com>
- Netlingo: <http://www.netlingo.com>
- Jargon File Resources: <http://www.tuxedo.org/~esr/jargon/jargon.html>

CGI	Common Gateway Interface; allows interaction between users and Websites through forms, orders, and other responses
FAQ	Frequently Asked Questions; usually covers points raised by newcomers; pronounced "fack"
HDML	handheld device markup language; formats content for Web-enabled mobile phones
HTML	hypertext markup language; code that tells a browser how to display text, graphics and other elements of a Web page
HTTP	hypertext transfer protocol
IP	Internet Protocol; a server address, often four numbers separated by dots: 123.45.678.910
MP3	MPEG audio layer 3; coding scheme for compressing audio files. MPEG stands for Motion Picture Experts Group.
PDF, pdf	portable document format (readable with Adobe Acrobat on any computer)
S-HTTP	Secure HTTP; sends an individual message in a secure, encrypted form

SSL	Secure Sockets Layer; encrypts data in multiple messages
TCP/IP	Transmission Control Protocol/Internet Protocol; basic software needed to connect to the Internet
URL	uniform resource locator; the address of a particular Website
WAP	Wireless Application Protocol; allows access to Web information over mobile phones, pagers, other devices
WML	Wireless Markup Language; an XML language used with WAP devices
XML	extensible markup language; an advanced Web language that allows designers to create their own tags to define, validate and interpret data

Punctuating abbreviations

Frequently used abbreviations tend to lose their periods — B.A. becomes BA, and U.S.A. becomes USA — but it's still correct to include them. As noted earlier, abbreviations with mixed capital and lower-case letters usually keep their periods. Mixed abbreviations that begin and end with capitals lose their periods. (Geographical abbreviations used in postal addresses should not include periods, however, because postal scanners have trouble with them. So snailmail addressed to British Columbia or California should display BC or CA with no punctuation.)

An honorific or title before a name is usually abbreviated (in North America, with a period; in Britain, without) when the person's whole name is included: Prof. Zhu Minhua, Maj. Gen. Robert Smith, Mr. David Porter, Ms. Joan Acosta. (But "Ms." often appears as "Ms" even in North America.)

A title does not appear before a name if a title follows the name: Louise Fairfax, MD; John Hutchinson, PhD.

When a sentence ends with an abbreviation including periods, only one period is needed: Welcome to B.C. When a sentence ends with a question mark or exclamation mark, it follows the last period of the abbreviation: Welcome to B.C.!

Pluralizing abbreviations

Simply add "s" to most abbreviations: MVPs (most valuable players), MIAs (soldiers missing in action), NGOs (nongovernmental organizations).

Abbreviating dates

International and governmental organizations tend to display dates as year/month/day: 1999/03/21 is March 21, 1999. Most people, however, prefer day/month/year (21 March 1999) or month/day/year (March 21, 1999). From 2001 to 2031, abbreviated dates may be ambiguous: does 03/04/05 mean April 5, 2003, March 4, 2005, or April 3, 2005?

To ensure understanding, write out dates in full or use abbreviations for the names of months: Apr 3 2005, 5 Apr 2003.

Abbreviations of calendar eras usually appear as:

AD: Anno Domini

BC: Before Christ

BP: Before the present (generally taken to be AD 2000 — so "6400 BP" = 4400 BC)

BCE: before the common era

CE: common era

These last two terms recognize that not everyone using the Christian calendar is necessarily a Christian.

Biased Terms

As a Webwriter you may want to challenge your readers, but challenges shouldn't include gratuitous pokes in the eye. Terms that seem perfectly natural to you may be deeply offensive to others. Is that because you're OK and your readers are thin-skinned idiots? Or because you don't have enough respect for your readers to address them in a civil manner?

Granted that concern with "political correctness" can lead to euphemism and denial of reality, I suggest that when you can use a term that doesn't bother your readers, you should choose it — especially if they themselves prefer the term. One happy result of this choice is likely to be better writing.

For example, the stereotyping that drives people crazy is sloppy writing that reflects (and promotes) sloppy thinking. Generalizations about any group — dumb college athletes, bad women drivers, violent teenagers, noisy American tourists — will invariably collapse under any serious examination.

So your Webtext should avoid such generalizations, whether you're tempted to make them about nationalities, ethnic groups, demographic groups, or any other class of people.

More specifically, consider the following guidelines for avoiding biased terms.

(a) *Pointless or irrelevant personal information.* The head of your company may be the mother of two, the skip of a curling team, a fan of F. Scott Fitzgerald, and a superb cook; none of that is relevant when she announces a stock split. Similarly, identifying a charged criminal as belonging to a particular ethnic group does little to enlighten your readers and may tend to make them draw unfounded generalizations.

(b) *Faint praise.* "Women are better than men at routine, repetitious jobs" not only insults men but suggests that women aren't very good at varied and creative work.

(c) *Gender bias.* In recent years, "gender" has come to mean the cultural or social roles assigned to men and women, while "sex" means the physiological or biological aspects of males and females. Many occupational terms have a "male" or "female" suffix because of ancient tradition, not modern reality. Changing "chairman" to "chairperson" isn't always adequate, in part because it sounds so self-conscious.

Consider the following alternatives:

actress:	actor (though only some actors are eligible for a "best actress" award)
alderman:	councillor (unless the term is official)
any man:	anyone, anybody
aviatrix:	flyer, pilot
anchorman/anchorwoman:	anchor
businessman/businesswoman:	business person, manager, entrepreneur, merchant
chairman/chairwoman:	chair, convenor, president
cleaning woman:	cleaner
common man:	average person
countryman:	compatriot
fireman:	firefighter
fisherman:	fisher (that may sound odd at first, but no one says "loggerman" or "carpenterman")
man a counter:	staff a counter, run a counter
man in the street:	ordinary people
mankind:	humanity, humans, people
man-made:	synthetic, artificial
manpower:	workforce, labor force, staff, personnel
policeman/policewoman:	police officer, constable, deputy (unless the officer's sex is relevant, as when a woman suspect is improperly searched by a policeman)

salesman/saleswoman:	sales representative, sales clerk, salesperson
stewardess:	flight attendant
waitress:	server, waiter
workman:	worker, employee

Gender bias can also turn up in singular pronouns: Anyone who bikes without a helmet will eventually get his head examined. The "generic" singular pronoun is supposed to be "he," but in practice we often prefer "they" — as in "get their head examined." This of course sounds a little odd; how can you have a plural pronoun and a singular noun?

While it doesn't work all the time, pluralizing the antecedent can solve many such problems: People who bike without helmets will eventually get their heads examined.

(d) *Sexual orientation.* "Gay" and "straight" were originally homosexual slang terms that have become standard usage. It's pointless to regret the loss of "gay" as a synonym for "happy," just as it's pointless to wish that "fond" still meant "foolish." While "gay" can apply to both men and women, you'll be clearer if you refer to "gay men and women" or to "gays and lesbians."

Be careful with terms that may be semantically loaded: "heterosexism" and "homophobia" are terms that criticize anti-gay attitudes, and you should use them only when you can back them up. Otherwise they're just name-calling, like "fag" and "dyke." Gays may feel free to use such terms about themselves, but outsiders should not.

"Transgendered" may mean either someone who lives as a member of the opposite sex, or someone who has actually changed sex. The latter may also be referred to as a "transsexual."

Don't confuse "sexual orientation" and "sexual preference." Sexual orientation has to do with whether one prefers people of one's own sex or not. Sexual preference has to do with preferring blonds or particular styles of making love.

(e) *Ethnic terms.* Be very careful about using terms like "ethnic," "race," and "visible minority." Yorkshire pudding is "ethnic" food just as kreplachs and papadams are. If you intend to mean "a group culturally and linguistically and physically different from the majority," you may still be on dangerous ground. Don't forget your readers may be reading your words in Karachi or Kyoto, where you would be the very visible minority.

When you must refer to people by ethnic and racial terms, use the terms they prefer: not Eskimo, but Inuit (singular Inuk); not Negro but African-American or black person. Should you capitalize words like "black"? Some people do, but "White" looks odd. Stick to using such terms as adjectives, not nouns, and you can usually stay in the lower case: a native attorney, a black poet.

Some terms, like "African," "Asian," or "Oriental" are so broad that they become meaningless. Berbers and Bantus are both Africans; Tamils and Japanese are both Asians; in the age of the Pacific Rim, the "Orient" is really to the west of most North Americans.

If a term like "native" seems odd to someone whose ancestors have lived in a country for ten generations, consider "aboriginal" or "indigenous." One Canadian term for "Native Indians" is "First Nations." Where possible, be as specific as possible: Not "A Montana Indian," but "A Montana Blackfoot."

(f) *Disabilities.* You're generally on safer ground with expressions like "a person with a disability" instead of "a disabled person" (which sounds as if the person isn't even conscious!).

When you refer to persons with physical or intellectual disabilities, avoid loaded terms like "victim," "afflicted with," or "suffering from." A child may use a wheelchair; the child should not be "confined" to the wheelchair. Be careful also to distinguish between disability and impairment (generally caused by accident or genetics) and disease.

In the case of intellectual disability and disease, use terms as accurately as possible. Pop psychology has made psychiatrists of us all, but don't use a term like "schizophrenic" or "bipolar" unless you really know what you're talking about. Again, put the term in a prepositional phrase: "a person with schizophrenia," or "people diagnosed with bipolar disorder."

(g) *Age*. North Americans are sensitive about their age, which may explain why we like euphemisms: "golden ager" rather than "old person," for example. Only an old person should feel free to use terms like "geezer" or "old fart," and even then it may be more distracting than amusing. Young people feel patronized by terms like "kid" or "youngster." Up to about the age of 16, they're boys and girls. After that they're men and women, or young persons. If a person's age is important to what you're writing about, mention it: John Chang, 19, is already a dot-com millionaire. At 79, Alma Jones is running in her 20th marathon. If age is irrelevant, don't bother with it.

Capitalization

Consult a dictionary or one of the styleguides mentioned for details on capitalization. What follows deals with some special cases that Webwriters should be aware of.

Capitalize trade names.

Someone left a Styrofoam cup and a box of Kleenex on the Xerox copier.

If Valium doesn't work, try a Zoloft. If that doesn't work, take an aspirin; in Canada, you should take an Aspirin.

NOTE: Companies holding trade names often prosecute writers who fail to capitalize them. This is to prevent the trade names from becoming generic and therefore available for anyone to use. This happened with brand names like Nylon, Lanolin, and Cellophane.

Similarly, follow the manufacturer's usage in capitalizing high-tech brand names, even when these include capitals within the word (also known derisively as "StudlyCaps").

WordPerfect

PowerPoint

SI/Metric units

Only the word Celsius takes a capital in Système International/metric terms.

10 km (kilometers)

50 g (grams)

10 ha (hectares)

25 mg (milligrams)

EXCEPTION: SI terms based on proper names take a capital, and so does the abbreviation for litre.

60 V (volts) — from Volta

100 G (gauss) — from Gauss

2 L (litres)

Capitalizing lists

If a bulleted list is grammatically part of the sentence that introduces it, listed items do not take capitals.

Chesterton offers you —

great skiing

superb snowboarding

exciting mountain biking

exhilarating whitewater rafting

awesome rock climbing

If the list is made up of complete sentences, each listed item does take a capital.

Why visit Chesterton?

It's got great skiing from November to April.

It's got superb snowboarding.

Mountain biking challenges everyone from novices to professionals.

Whitewater rafting is the best in the country.

Rock climbing is awesome, but not for the faint-hearted.

Compound Words

When a new term, made up of two or more words, comes into the language, we usually write it as separate words — for example, electronic mail, or Web site. But we soon hyphenate it or shorten it, or both. Electronic mail soon became e-mail, and has already become email for many of its users. "Web site" is still common, but many people prefer Website. "Web-site" is very rare.

While practice does vary on the Web, the following compound-word usages appear to be preferred by most current users:

email

Web page

Website

Webwriter

In many cases, hyphens help to make our meaning clear, and we'd better hang on to them. Consider, for example:

I resent your message.

I re-sent your message.

In the same manner, do we want more advanced research (additional programs like present advanced research), or more-advanced research (programs that go beyond what we're doing now)? Was she wearing a light brown coat or a light-brown coat? Is he an old computer expert (aged but technically up to date), or an old-computer expert (capable of fixing a Lisa?).

Many compound terms, when they serve as adjectives, take hyphens:

a 50-year-old rock climber

our day-to-day routine

she joined a well-established firm

When we turn such phrases around, we drop the hyphens:

the rock climber is 50 years old

we follow the same routine from day to day

her firm is well established

Exceptions

When a compound phrase contains an "ly" adverb, don't use a hyphen:

an insanely great computer

a truly astounding event

the triumphantly grinning winner

And don't hyphenate a compound containing a comparative or superlative:

She is the least known but most influential editor in the city.

Flash is one of the more dramatic tools for Web creation.

Doubtful Terms

The following expressions are either clichés, trying to become clichés, or plain bad English. They may sound fresh and unusual the first time you hear them, but (to use a cliché) they get old fast. Instead of expanding awareness, such terms make it harder to think clearly and accurately about the ideas they represent. If you feel you must use them, at least think carefully about why they're necessary to your Webtext, and what effect they're likely to have on your readers.

The Web itself has generated a number of clichés and trite expressions. Precisely because the Web changes so rapidly, such expressions look very dated very soon. Some of them, though, are pretty funny when you first understand them. In the following list, they appear with an asterisk.

24-7 (= 24 hours a day, 7 days a week)

*404 (someone who doesn't know anything — from "404 Not Found" response on seeking a URL)

Actualize

*Adminisphere (people above the rank and file of any organization)

Alot (= A lot). Bad English.

*Alpha geek (an organization's top computer expert)

Alright (should always be All right). Bad English.

And I'm all like...

*And more! (If the rest of the attractions aren't enough, this won't help)

Anything for dummies

Anything from hell

Anything R Us

Apples and oranges

As if!

Award-winning

Awesome

*Back to home page (if a search engine has brought them straight to this page, your readers can't go "back" to somewhere they've never been)

Ballpark figure

Basically

Begs the question (Bad English when used to mean "raises the question")

Between a rock and a hard place

Big time!

*Blamestorming (deciding as a group who was responsible for something that went wrong)

Bleeding edge

*Blowing your buffer (losing your train of thought)

*Bookmark (remember someone for future reference)

Bottom line

*Bozon (basic unit of stupidity)

*Brain fart (information off the top of an expert's head)

Breakthrough (especially "major breakthrough")

Build it and they will come

Buzzword

Can of worms

Cash cow

Celeb

*Check out... (Prefer "Visit" or "See")

Cheesy

Chichi

Chicken soup for anyone

*Chips and salsa (hardware and software)

*Circling the drain (winding down doomed projects)

Classy

*Cobweb site (Website never updated)

Concern (= problem)

Consensus of opinion

Criteria (used as singular)

*Cutting edge

Cut to the chase

Cyber-anything

*Dancing baloney (irrelevant animations that add nothing to a Website)

*Dead tree version (text on paper); also, treeware

Deal with it!

Deconstruct

Decouple

Deep pockets

Deja vu all over again

*Digerati (those who are very computer literate)

*Digitocracy (those who are actually making money from the Web)

*Dilberted (exploited by one's bosses in a notably insane way)

*Dog and pony show (demonstration of a new application)

*Docubug (mistake in the documentation)

*Domainism (judging someone by their email address — especially America Online)

Doh, Duh

Done deal

Don't go there

Downsize (and any other euphemism for "fire employees")

Dysfunctional

*E-biz, e-tail

Eatery

Edgy

*Ego surfing (looking for mentions of oneself on the Web)

Empowered

End result

*Enhanced (Usually means viewable in only one browser because the site creator didn't know — or care — enough to make it look right in all browsers)

Euro-anything

Evolving your company

F-word

Facilitate

Flame (extreme insults delivered over email, often over trivial matters)

Gathering (= meeting)

*Geekosphere (personal area around your computer)

Get over it!

Get with the program

Give me a break

*Glazing (losing interest in what one is hearing or seeing)

Go ballistic

Go postal

*Graybar land (wasting time while your browser slowly downloads a big file)

Growing your business

Hellloooo?

Hissy fit

Holistic anything

*Hourglass mode (like graybar land: waiting for a slow computer to complete some task)

Hyper-anything

Idiot's guide to anything

I hear that!

I'm like (= I said)

Incredible (= good)

In denial

Influencers

In your face!

Irregardless. Bad English.

Issue (= problem)

It goes without saying (so why say it?)

*Jargonaut (someone who overwhelms listeners and readers with techie jargon)

*Keyboard plaque (the dirt that builds up on computer keyboards)

*Kewl (an attempt to sound cool without sounding naïve)

Kudos (Greek for "praise" — if you must use it, remember that it's singular, not plural. No one ever got a single "kudo.")

Level playing field

Light at the end of the tunnel

Like herding cats

Like nailing Jell-O to the wall

Like there's no tomorrow

*Link rot (loss of connections when sites go offline or move their URLs)

Luddite (meaning anyone who dislikes computers)

*Meatspace (physical reality)

*Mouse droppings (dust and gunk inside one's mouse)

*Mouse potato
(someone immobilized in front of a computer)

Movers and shakers

Multi-tasking

Needless to say (then why say it?)

Neo-anything

Nerd

*Newbie (a newcomer to any field, especially computers and the Web)

No problem (= you're welcome)

...Not!

Online buying experience

Paradigm

Parameters

*PEBCAK (problem exists between chair and keyboard: the user has screwed up)

*Percussive maintenance (restoring a computer's functions by hitting it)

Per se (means "as such," so use the English expression)

Personal opinion

*Point your browser (Browsers don't have points — prefer "Go to...")

Politically correct

Postmodern, Pomo

Power anything

Preaching to the choir

Pro-active

Puh-leeze!

Reinvent the wheel

Retarded

Retro

Rubric

Sassy

Segue

Self-actualizing

*Shovelware (something dumped online without even an attempt to adapt it to the medium)

Singing from the same hymn book

*Snailmail (ordinary mail delivery)

*SoHo (small office, home office)

Solution (= computer product)

*Square-headed girlfriend (a computer)

Sucks

Synergize

Tacky

Tasked with

Task force (= committee)

Techno-anything

The ultimate anything

*This site under construction (if so, it shouldn't be accessible until complete)

Throw money at the problem

Tip of the iceberg

To die for

To partner

Total anything

Ultra-anything

*Uninstalled (fired)

Up close and personal

Utilize (prefer "use" every time)

Veggies

Virtual anything

Wake-up call

Way cool

Way hot

*Wetware (brain)

Whatever!

Window of opportunity

Win-win

World class

*World Wide Wait (the Web)

Yeah, right

You go, girl!

You rock!

You the man!

*Zen mail (email with headers but no text in the message body)

Measurements & Numerical Terms

Americans are the predominant users of the Web, and Americans also use a medieval measurement system abandoned by every other civilized nation. The "Système international d'unités" (SI) is the generally accepted version of the metric system. As a Webwriter you should be able to supply measurement terms that are meaningful to both Americans and the other 5.7 billion people on the planet.

If your Website needs to present measurements, and you expect readers from all over the world, you should display terms in both SI and "imperial" units.

Numbers in general

In most cases, use words for numbers below 10, and numerals for numbers above 10:

> seven days, 14 links, one and only, 11 men to a side

If a number begins a sentence, always spell it out:

> Fifteen men sat on a dead man's chest.

> Six dollars will get you a ticket.

But if a number is part of an address, a title, a brand, or an organization's name, follow its usage even at the beginning of a sentence:

> 195 Kinloch Lane was at the end of the street.

> 7Up is a popular soft drink.

> 4587 Corporation is a little-known holding company.

When providing two different sets of numbers, use words for one and numerals for the other:

> We have 6 two-bedroom suites, 1 studio apartment, and 4 three-bedroom suites.

Use a hyphen when writing out numbers between 21 and 99:

Thirty-nine students crammed the classrom.

One hundred and sixty-two emails arrived overnight.

Don't use commas with long, spelled-out numbers or mixed numbers:

Pay to the order of John Smith: One thousand two hundred fifty-five dollars.

He stands six feet 11 inches tall.

He covered the course in one hour 15 minutes 16 seconds.

Imperial/traditional units of measurement

Traditional units can be confusing, especially to international readers. A Canadian gallon, for example, is larger than an American gallon. If you must use traditional measurement units, try to be consistent; where your readers might need metric equivalents, be sure to supply them. Also, try to avoid mixing metric and traditional units: In Canada, where metric hasn't been fully adopted, people tend to write: "I paid 73 cents a litre for gas, and my car gets only 15 miles per gallon."

Here is a table of some common traditional units of measurement and their metric equivalents. Note that traditional-unit abbreviations usually take periods, while metric abbreviations do not.

Name/Abbreviation	Metric Equivalent
1 pound/lb.	454 g
1 ounce/oz.	28 g
1 US ton/ton	907 kg
1 imperial ton/ton	1016 kg
1 inch/in.	2.5 cm
1 foot/ft.	0.3 m
1 mile/mi.	1.6 km

1 square foot/sq. ft.	0.09 m^2
1 yard/yd.	0.91 m
1 acre/acre	4047 m^2
1 acre/acre	0.40 ha (hectares)
1 cubic foot/ft.	0.02 m^3
1 US gallon/gal.	3.78 L
1 imperial gallon/gal.	4.54 L
50 degrees Fahrenheit/°F	10°C

SI Numerals

When using SI terms in technical material, use a combination of numerals and abbreviations: 1.6 km, NOT 1.6 kilometres. In other material, use numerals with spelled-out units: Drive 10 kilometres south from the bridge and follow the signs to the vineyard. Do NOT use spelled-out words and SI abbreviations (ten km).

In SI usage, a space replaces the comma in numbers with five or more digits:

50 000 votes

$145 000

The space is optional with four digits:

1 152 votes

1152 votes

If four- and five-digit numbers are mixed, all should have a space:

Our opponents spent $9 000 while we spent $10 500.

SI measurements include some units that aren't really SI, including time. What follows is a list of measurements and their abbreviations, which you should present consistently.

Name	Symbol	Quantity
ampere	A	electric current
bel	B	sound intensity
coulomb	C	electric charge
degree Celsius	°C	temperature
hectare	ha	area (100 square meters)
hertz	Hz	frequency
kelvin	K	temperature
kilogram	kg	weight (2.2 pounds)
knot	kn	1,852 meters per hour
litre	L	volume
meter	m	length
minute	'	plane angle
minute	min	time
nautical mile	M	1,852 m (marine distance)
second	"	plane angle
tonne	t	1,000 kg (2,200 pounds)

Online Advice About Online Writing Style

Here are some Websites that offer good advice about writing for the Web. Such sites usually offer still more links to additional resources. You can also find more resources by using search engines and keying in phrases like "Web style" or "Webwriting" or "writing for the Web" (include the double quotation marks around multi-word phrases.)

- Tim Berners-Lee's CERN Style Guide: <http://www.w3.org/Provider/Style/Introduction.html>

- Jakob Nielsen: <http://www.useit.com/papers/webwriting/>

- Jutta Degener on writing and editing for the Web: <http://kbs.cs.tu-berlin.de/~jutta/ht/writing.html>

- Yale Center for Advanced Instructional Media Web Style Guide: <http://info.med.yale.edu/caim/manual/>

- Bookmarks for Webwriting: <http://www.shef.ac.uk/misc/personal/lb1sen/bookmark/webmarks.html>

- Resources on Web style: <http://www.westegg.com/badpages/>

- Joe Gillespie's Web Page Design for Designers: <http://www.wpdfd.com/wpdhome.htm>

- Jeffrey Zeldman's Ask Dr. Web: <http://www.zeldman.com/faq.html>

- Web Pages that Suck: <http://webpagesthatsuck.com>

- Webmaster — Webwriting Style Resources: <http://www.cio.com/central/style.html>

- David Siegel's Net Tips for Writers and Designers (Web Wonk): <http://www.dsiegel.com/tips/index.html>

- World Wide Web Unleashed (Web updates for print book): <http://www.december.com/works/wwwu.html>

- Creating Killer Websites Online (Web updates for print book): <http://www.killersites.com/core.html>

Case Study 1: Editing Scrolling Articles

An Audience of One

Strong editing can help even an article designed for scrolling. Here's a case in point — an article from WebWord, a site created to help writers. After it first appeared, I responded with a suggested edit to the coauthor, John S. Rhodes, who kindly allowed me to present both versions of the text in this book. My suggestions are in square brackets in the edited version.

Visit the WebWord site at <http://www.WebWord.com>.

Consider this article again in Chapter 8 when we discuss advocacy on the Web. It dramatizes the difficulty you face as a Webwriter trying to make a carefully reasoned argument. The methods that work so well on paper can actually undercut your persuasiveness by making jolt-hungry readers impatient. The authors have helped by creating subheads to prepare readers for shifts in their argument, but assertion still works better on the Web than building a case fact by fact.

Original version

WebWord.com : Moving WebWord : Designing for an Audience of One — User vs. Users (8-31-98)

Designing for an Audience of One

by John S. Rhodes and Bill Skeet

If you want a great Website, one that custom fits each person, then read on.

You think you know all about usability and you think you understand your users. You feel like you know them

Edited version

WebWord.com : Moving WebWord : Designing for an Audience of One — User vs. Users (8-31-98)

Designing for an Audience of One

by John S. Rhodes and Bill Skeet

You want a great Website that custom-fits each person.

You know all about usability and you understand your users. You know their demographics, their favorite Web

dead cold, right on. You have solid demographic information, you know their favorite Web pages, you have data on when they are visiting your site and what they are buying. You know a lot, but we bet you are looking at averages.

Are you also looking at data points? Are you looking at individuals?

One Size Does Not Fit All

Simply stated, the problem is that you lose individuals for the sake of knowing the group averages. You're designing for the common denominator when you could be designing your site to fit each and every person. Further, you could be marketing one-to-one — making each interaction personalized.

The Web allows you to communicate with each and every user. Simply put, your site always interfaces with individuals. Groups of people are not looking at your site, it is a one-at-a-time situation. Think about it, when was the last time a group of users bought something from your site?

pages, when they visit your site, and what they buy.

You know a lot, but we bet you are looking at averages.

One Size Does Not Fit All

Simply stated, you're designing for the common denominator when you could be designing your site to fit each person. Further, you could be marketing one-to-one — personalizing each interaction.

Your site always interfaces with individuals. When was the last time a group of users bought something from your site?

Average Person Fallacy

Maybe you think you're on top of the situation just described. Maybe you're designing a site so the "average person" can use it.

There is a well-established adage in human factors that the average person does not exist. For example, the result of designing for the body dimensions of the so-called average person is that the smaller 50 percent of the users cannot reach the controls or read the displays, and the larger 50 percent will not have room to move about comfortably.

No one is average. In fact, few people are average in even a few dimensions (see *Human Performance Engineering,* 1996, by Robert W. Bailey).

To test the concept of the average person, a 1952 anthropometric study categorized 4,063 men according to ten measurements used in clothing design. Not one man was average in all ten dimensions and less than 4 percent were average in even the first three.

Average Person Fallacy

Maybe you think you're on top of the situation just described. Maybe you're designing a site so the "average person" can use it.

But no one is average. In fact, few people are average in even a few dimensions (see *Human Performance Engineering,* 1996, by Robert W. Bailey). *[We could use more publishing data, maybe a Web link.]*

This means that designing a Website requires more than imagining what a faceless, "average" user might do. It means you must identify real users — their motivations, abilities, skills, needs, biases, and environments.

Of course you can't build a custom site for every user. But you can define your audience as precisely as possible. Then, try to identify the characteristics of that population. You need a good sample, and you need to look at the data points as well as the averages. *[Should you define "data points"?]*

This means that designing a Website requires more than imagining what a faceless, generic user might do. It means you must identify real users — their motivations, abilities, skills, needs, biases, and environments. Find out what makes each person tick.

Of course, it is impossible to build a custom site for every single user. The key for making this a manageable problem is to define your audience as precisely as possible. Then, try to identify the characteristics of that population. You need a good sample, and you need to look at the data points as well as the averages.

The Website design should accommodate 95 percent of your users by considering a full range of characteristics from the 2.5th percentile to the 97.5th percentile. Here is a partial list of characteristics you could consider:

- Language (e.g., English)
- Visual acuity (and color-blindness)
- Internet connection speed
- Browser type and version
- Time constraints

The Website design should accommodate 95 percent of your users by considering a full range of characteristics from the 2.5th percentile to the 97.5th percentile. *[Why this range? Why not settle for 90 or 85 percent?]* Here is a partial list of characteristics you could consider:

- Language (e.g., English)
- Visual acuity (and color-blindness)
- Internet connection speed
- Browser type and version
- Time constraints
- Occupation
- Technical knowledge

Obviously there are many more. Define what characteristics are important according to the needs of your site. For example, is your target user weak on technical knowledge, and therefore likely to need clear, nontechnical language?

- Occupation
- Technical knowledge

Obviously there are many more. Define what characteristics are important according to the needs of your site.

Building Custom Fitting Websites

The usability of a site will suffer if you take an "audience view" of content development and site design. The language that you use should make your site sound and feel like a one-to-one, personal conversation.

Think about how much a lecture sucks compared to a personal conversation. Design the site as if you were interacting with a single person.

Besides using a conversational tone, there are at least three other ways to improve the site-to-user interaction.

First, while controversial, you can use cookies. People are becoming more familiar with them and hence their comfort level with them has risen. Also note that your competitors are probably using them, and if you don't you can suffer from a competitive disadvantage.

Building Custom Fitting Websites

The usability of a site will suffer if you take an "audience view" of content development and site design. The language that you use should make your site sound and feel like a one-to-one, personal conversation. So design the site as if you were interacting with a single person.

Besides using a conversational tone, you have at least three other ways to improve site-to-user interaction.

First, while cookies are controversial, people are becoming more familiar with them and hence less suspicious about them. Your competitors are probably using them, and if you don't you can suffer from a competitive disadvantage. *[Explain why.]*

Second, conduct a survey. Individuals will tell you a surprising

105

Another way to improve site-to-user interaction is to conduct a survey. Individuals divulge a surprising amount. Note that this method is only advocated if you use this information strictly for the purposes of improving your site.

You can also attend to individual users via email. Never underestimate how far a quick response to an email will go. Be sure to take great strides to quickly and effectively respond. You can gain the trust of users extremely fast this way, and it is much easier than changing the Website. Also be sure to encourage feedback.

The bottom line is that you can build sites that are more personalized. Think beyond groups. Think about each person that is visiting your site. It is a one-to-one world baby.

[794 words]

amount. You must, however, use this information strictly to improve your site — not to provide marketing information for others.

Never underestimate the user's pleasure in getting a quick response to email. You can gain user trust extremely fast this way, and it is much easier than changing the Website. Also be sure to encourage feedback.

Yes, you can build more personalized sites. Think beyond groups. Think about each person who is visiting your site. Just like the days of your life, deal with them one at a time.

[584 words]

Case Study 2: Chunking a Text

Imagine that you're creating content for the "Cataract Home Page," a site designed to provide information and help for people dealing with this widespread eye problem. You find the following article, which you think is worth putting on the site, but it runs 800 words and has some local political content that really isn't relevant to your purposes. As you read it, think about how you might cut it and break it into chunks of no more than 100 words. Then test your version against the one provided after the full article.

Last spring the vision in my left eye became suddenly worse. Aware that aging eyes can deteriorate rapidly, I went in for an exam and a new prescription.

"A new prescription won't do you any good," the doctor told me, "until you have that cataract out."

In more ways than one, that diagnosis led me to clearer sight — not only visually, but politically. I see much better now, but I don't always like what I see.

My first choice was to go on a waiting list for eye surgery, or to pay over a thousand dollars to do it at once in a private clinic. I listened to the clinic's pitch — no waiting, newer equipment — and said thanks, I'd wait my turn.

By the autumn, night driving was getting worrisome. Oncoming headlights flared at me. Sodium streetlights looked like mocking orange images of the cataract. Any kind of work in dim light became impossible. I was using my right eye exclusively, but eventually my brain couldn't edit out the message from my left eye, and a kind of ghostly blur formed in my field of vision. With the right eye closed, I was effectively blind.

Of course I learned a lot during these months: that if we live long enough, we all get cataracts. That replacing the blurry organic lens with a plastic one is now a routine operation. A news report cheered me up with the news that the world looks "clean and blue" after a cataract removal.

Still, I wasn't looking forward to it. After a lifetime of nearsightedness, I was anxious about anything affecting my vision; the idea of a scalpel in my eyeball, under only local anesthetic, inspired plenty of morbid fantasies.

In mid-November, I went into my local hospital's day-surgery waiting room at nine in the morning. A tedious two hours followed while I lay in bed getting drops in my eyes. Then, feeling like a bit player in some TV medical epic, I was wheeled into an operating room and offered my choice of soothing CDs to listen to.

Baroque music first provided a background to a disturbing conversation between two nurses getting ready to assist at the operation. Once they had parked me on the operating table and tucked a couple of pillows under my knees, they considered which American states would be best for emigrating Canadian nurses. I gathered that Colorado, for one, doesn't require a written exam before such a nurse can go to work. This was not idle chatter but serious career planning.

The operation itself was almost painless. The local anesthetic worked with amazing speed, and before long I was watching a kind of light show: swirls of yellow, pink, and black filled my field of vision as the surgeon worked. Almost before I knew it, I was back in the reception area with a cup of coffee, a carrot muffin, and a patch on my eye. Another candidate for the same procedure was telling a nurse: "I'm afraid I might flinch." Don't worry, I wanted to tell him. You'll be too scared to flinch.

At noon, an hour after the operation began, I was dressed and out in the waiting room, where my wife soon collected me. By the time we reached home I was feeling pretty rocky, and spent the afternoon trying to sleep. While I had no appetite for dinner, by nine that night I was reading my email, my nose almost pressed against the monitor.

When the patch came off the next morning, I was astonished to see clearly without my glasses on. The new lens has made my left eye — formerly the worse one by far — much the better one. At close range, people and objects are almost surreally clear.

And the news story was right: when I use my left eye, colors really are cleaner and bluer. Even when they don't form cataracts, our lenses imperceptibly turn yellow as they age. The operation was like cleaning a windowpane after years of neglect.

I was one of four cataract patients that day in a medium-size suburban hospital. We may be the lucky ones. Growing numbers of aging Canadians will need this procedure and many others. As health-care funding fails, and health professionals head for Colorado and other parts of the world, what will we do? Will older people have to fight political wars just for the chance to see again? Or will we be just another "special interest group," making unfair demands on our clear-eyed, tax-burdened, deficit-fighting fellow-citizens? Will we end up like Shelley's king — "old, mad, blind, despised and dying"?

I have no answers. But with my colder, clearer vision I now appreciate more than ever that "wisdom" comes from an ancient word for "sight." And I see the wisdom in Jonathan Swift's adage that "There's none so blind as they that won't see."

If I were editing this piece into chunks for a cataract-information site, I'd delete all the political references and break it into three chunks: Early Symptoms, The Operation, and Operation Aftermath. Visitors to the site could then see a link something like this:

A Typical Cataract Operation: Read about <u>Early Symptoms, The Operation,</u> and <u>Operation Aftermath</u>. You'll find it's less scary than you thought!

Early Symptoms

Night driving was difficult, and any kind of work in dim light became impossible. I was using my right eye exclusively, but eventually a ghostly blur, the message from my left eye, formed in my field of vision. Closing my right eye made me effectively blind.

I learned that we all get cataracts if we live long enough, and replacing the cataract with a plastic lens is now routine. A news report cheered me up by promising the world would look "clean and blue" afterward. (85 words)

The Operation

After arrival at the hospital at nine one morning, I lay in bed receiving eye drops for two hours. They then wheeled me into the operating room and made me comfortable. I even got to choose the background music.

The operation itself was almost painless. The local anesthetic worked fast and I watched a kind of light show: swirls of yellow, pink, and black filled my sight while the surgeon worked. Almost before I knew it, I was back in the reception area with a cup of coffee, a carrot muffin, and a patch on my eye. (97 words)

Operation Aftermath

At noon, an hour after the operation began, I was on my way. Feeling rocky, I tried to sleep that afternoon. While I had no appetite for dinner, by that evening I was reading my email.

When the patch came off next morning, I was astonished to see clearly without my glasses on. The new lens has made my left eye — formerly the worse one — much the better one. At close range, people and objects are almost surreally clear. Colors really are cleaner and bluer. Removing a cataract is like cleaning a windowpane after years of neglect. (98 words)

Comment: Note that even in chunks, text can benefit from short paragraphs — even subheadings can help within a single chunk. If I decided to keep some of the political commentary after all, I'd still try for a maximum of a hundred words per chunk. Or I might include a fourth link: <u>Full text of original article</u>. Either way, I'd have given my readers as many choices as possible in obtaining the information they were seeking, in whatever sequence they preferred.

Exercise 4: Editing for Clear, Short Webtext

Here is a passage that needs serious revision. Try to reduce it to a maximum of 100 words (the length of a typical chunk), or preferably less. If that seems impossible, try to break it into no more than two chunks, each with its own title. Compare your version with the one at the back of the book.

Chesterton, after decades first as a logging town and mining center, and then as a seriously depressed community that very nearly became a ghost town, is now making a comeback as a major tourist destination. Beginning in 1891 as a company town built by the Chesterton Logging Company, the town grew to become a thriving community of over 3,000 men, women, and children. During World War I, the population grew still more to meet the demand for spruce to build airplanes, so the population rose to almost 4,000. After the war, a zinc mine went into operation at the base of Mount Freeman (named for pioneer trapper Daniel Freeman, who conducted an exploration of the region in the 1820s). The conduct of mining operations resulted in great prosperity in the late 1920s, even after the Chesterton sawmill shut down. But then with the Great Depression the zinc market collapsed and hundreds of workers lost their jobs. Chesterton's population shrank to not much more than 300 souls; the town was at death's door. After World War II, however, the creation of Chesterton Regional Park brought about a new rebirth for the town. As tourism began to grow, the community found a new lease on life catering to skiers, hikers, and campers. In the past 10 or 20 years, Chesterton has seen development of world-class skiing at High Corniche, the North American Kayak Championships at Roaring Creek, and a booming whitewater rafting business that puts almost 200 rafts into the Old Horse River every summer season. With 1,200 year-round residents, Chesterton is now a major recreation center and eco-tourism destination. Click here for details on accommodations and recreation facilities.

[277 words]

Exercise 4 — continued

_____

_____

_____

_____

_____

_____

_____

_____

_____

_____

_____

_____

_____

_____

_____

_____

_____

_____

_____

Exercise 5: Editing a News Release

Many organizations archive their news releases for months or years. They're not news anymore, but they can still be history. Take the following news release and edit it twice: first, just to correct errors and make it shorter and easier to read, and second, to appear as a "What's New" item — just the basic story — while the event is still in the near future.

> The Chesterton Folk Music Society will stage the first ever Chesterton Folk Music Festival at Green River Park on July 5, 6, and 7. The event will feature an opening-night concert by Cajun singer-songwriter Marc Belliveau, who's latest CD has just been released. Other singers and groups will include Carolyn Loewen, Dora Hardy, and the Mexican women's quartet Las Golondrinas. The Green River Gang, our own local folk trio, will also perfomr. Many local ethnic restaurants will serve food at booths in the park: New Tandoori, Pancho's Villa, East Garden, Pyrogy House, and Little Singapore. The Society estimates that 20,000 people will attend at least part of the festival. "We're really exited about the event," says Folk Music Society president Mary O'Reilley. "Four three day's, Chesterton will be the center of the folk world." Tickets will be $50 for all three days, or $25/day.

[144 words]

_____

_____

_____

_____

_____

_____

Exercise 5 — continued

_____

_____

_____

_____

_____

_____

_____

_____

_____

_____

_____

_____

_____

_____

_____

_____

_____

_____

_____

6
CORPORATE WEBWRITING

While the writing principles discussed in this book apply to all Websites, writing text for corporate sites is different in some ways than writing for noncorporate sites. A corporate Website reflects the consensus of a formal group — a company, a university, a government agency — about how it ought to present itself on the Web. A commercial Website for a retail outlet or Webzine, for example, is more likely to reflect a single individual's vision, whether quirky or conformist. A corporate Website is the result of a lot of meetings, and the input from a lot of sources may or may not help those who actually put the site together.

Admittedly, a corporate site may also reflect a single person's vision — if that person can sell it to the rest of the group creating the Website. But in general, a corporate site is usually a compromise of some kind. If you are the Webwriter for such a group, you face a host of largely political challenges in turning those compromises into good writing.

Challenges for Corporate Webwriters

Your first challenge as a corporate Webwriter is to make your group understand what the Web can and cannot do, and how a Website can further the group's interests. If you are also the group's Webmaster, you presumably have the technical understanding of the Web's requirements. You accept that part of your job is to educate your group about those requirements, and your group will usually take your word as final. But it may be harder to explain to them the text requirements of a good Website. You can explain how the writing on your group's site can exploit the Web while avoiding its pitfalls, but it may take a while to make your message understood. Most of us, after all, defer to the HTML guru. But most of us also think "anyone can write," so opinions on Website content are easy to get.

What if you're not the Webmaster, and the group has called you in after accepting the technical suggestions of a nonwriter? Then you could have a problem, because the designer may have been concerned with technical questions of display, not with the principles of Orientation, Information, and Action.

As a Webwriter you may face yet another tangle: Your group may not have a consensus on what its own interests are and how the Website will advance them. Very often, groups automatically adopt the old-fashioned communication model of the FedEx courier, delivering a message against all odds to a passive recipient whose only part in the process is to sign for the package. They aren't thinking about the "you" attitude discussed in Chapter 2: Good Webwriting expresses ideas in terms of the reader's advantage. Too often, groups want to go onto the Web to talk only about how wonderful and important they are — not about how they can make themselves useful to their readers.

Marijke Rijsberman, a Webwriter for a Silicon Valley consulting firm, puts it this way:

> The company decides (and lots of companies are deciding the same thing) that [Web] content should be taken care of in the marketing department, as the gaggle of talent and experience most pertinent to the task. But the thing marketing departments typically do is take care of the "message" — what we want others to know about the company, whether or not they want to know about the company. The basic mindset is that of advertising: breaking into the awareness of people who are not looking for the information we want them to have.
>
> I suppose the model works for banner ads. But it does not work for other writing on the Web, which needs to recognize that

people come looking for you. Of course, they don't come looking for ads, they come on the general assumption that the Web is an information-rich medium that may contain the answers to their questions. So yes, they may want to know about your company, but chances are that they really want information that's within the company's expertise and they want that information much more than the stuff you put in the corporate brochure.

Web analyst and engineer Jakob Nielsen argues that most corporate Websites are not just failures, but are actively damaging to their creators' reputations. While he focuses on commercial sites, I think his findings are equally true for other group-sponsored sites.

The evidence Nielsen offers is pretty devastating. He cites one study of 15 big commercial Websites in which users could find information only 42 percent of the time, even though they started from the home page each time. In another study, three out of five online shoppers had given up trying to find the item they wanted to buy. A third survey found that, out of 20 major sites, simple Website organization principles (for example, "Is the site organized by user goals?") were observed only half the time.

"The odds are against any company that wants to put up a Website," says Nielsen. "In my estimate, 90 percent of commercial Websites have poor usability."

This failure rate is all the more baffling because the decision-makers are usually very focused on pleasing customers in ordinary marketplaces. Imagine a car dealership where you couldn't find a car (or a sales rep) on the lot, or a supermarket where you couldn't find the fresh produce or the checkout stands. Imagine a loan officer who bragged about the bank's assets, but never asked about your own financial needs.

Much of the problem with corporate Websites is poor structure: visitors receive inadequate orientation, so they can't navigate to the information they want. And of course, if they don't have the information, they won't perform the action desired of them by the group running the site: to buy the product, to join the party, to apply for admission to the college.

But even when the site design is good, the quality of the writing may make the information unusable and the desired action unappealing to most readers.

Define Your Audience

A corporate site should reach a wide range of readers without trying to be all things to all people. A college site should address students (potential and enrolled), faculty, support staff, potential employees, and employers. A bank should address its own staff, its current and potential customers, and the business community. A municipal government site addresses its residents and taxpayers, its staff, and potential investors. All corporate sites should of course address the general public as well, but they will do that best by showing they know how to address their specific audiences.

In some cases, the site may invite particular readers to pages created just for them. Many companies, for example, list Job Opportunities as a link on their front page. Pages intended strictly for internal use by staff can be password protected.

Large organizations may be able to afford intensive research into their audiences, which of course will help them focus their Website. In any case, it's important that a corporate site express a consistent tone that is appropriate to its intended audiences. (I discuss semantics and register in Chapter 8.) That means achieving a consensus within your organization both about your audience and about the best way to address it.

Corporate Webwriting Needs the "You" Attitude

In Chapter 3, I mentioned the "FedEx" communication model. Until fairly recently, most people — including writers — grew up learning to communicate in school and the workplace using that model, which assumes an active sender and a passive receiver for every message. The message itself is a lump of information that the receiver accepts like a downloaded file. The standard metaphors for this model are either postal (Get the message?) or ballistic (We're targeting the 18-to-35 demographic).

The technical term for this model is "instrumental," because it works on the passive receiver like a crowbar or baseball bat, to create a specific desired response. The implicit message in this model is "Do what I say."

The instrumental FedEx model works fine in media like print, radio, or TV. That's because the receiver has little or no chance to respond beyond a letter to the editor or a phone call to a talk-back line. Communication is effectively one-way.

But as I argued in Chapter 3, the Web really runs on a much more sophisticated "constructivist" model, in which both sides constantly change roles — sending and receiving at virtually the same time, adapting each message in the light of the last response. Both parties "construe" the meaning of the exchange, and it may end with both sides in unexpected territory, knowing things they didn't expect to know. The metaphor here is the conversation, and the implicit message is "Is this what you want?"

Even the old FedEx model expects the receiver to sign for the package, or regurgitate the lecture, or vote as the spin doctor wishes. But it's still a vertical relationship between the boss and the bossed. On the Web, relationships are far more horizontal, and anyone who doesn't care to be bossed can escape with the click of a mouse.

And *that* message, to use a ballistic metaphor, has still not penetrated the thick skulls of many Web sponsors — even the businesses that live or die by pleasing their customers. The message on their sites is pure ego: We do this, we do that, we can make you happy, so make us happy by doing what we want you to do.

The Canadian scholar Northrop Frye once distinguished between "ego art" and "self art." Ego art sees everyone as a worshipful audience for the ego's own splendor; the only purpose of the audience is to admire the perfect, unchangeable, yet always-insecure ego. Self art, by contrast, wants to provoke a response from other selves, to learn and change. The self, being secure, doesn't fear change — or challenge.

In business, good writing requires a "you" attitude that concentrates solely on the customer and the customer's needs. You don't even say: "We have a great deal for you, so do what we say" — you say: "You can take advantage of a great deal, if this is the deal you want." In other words, the constructivist, self-art model is interactive, a conversation with the reader/customer rather than an egomaniac's monologue.

So in the interactive medium of the Web, writers *must* keep their own egos offstage, and engage the reader on terms of equality and shared interests. The Webwriter expects to learn as well as teach, to buy as well as sell —

to move and to be moved. Such writing entails not fulsome, manipulative flattery but a nonverbal message of respect and interest. A site that's slow to load and hard to navigate is an ego site. A quick-loading site with good navigation reflects a self site, considerate of readers. Webtext that's precious or bombastic may say a lot about the writer's big vocabulary, but it speaks much more loudly of the writer's big ego.

Even if we grew up as writers in the FedEx world of print on paper, we need to recognize that the old model doesn't work here. Our readers may not know instrumentalism from constructivism, but they know when they're getting respect and when they're not. On the Web they enjoy a power of response that we ignore at our peril. But if we remember the "you" attitude and engage them in a genuine dialogue (as *The Cluetrain Manifesto* argues we should), we will all profit from every online conversation.

Too Many Webwriters Can Spoil the Site

Bureaucracies, whether corporate or governmental, can make life hard for the Webwriter. Web designer Stephen Martin has seen what can happen when an organization allows too many people to do their own thing on its Website:

> In the government world (and on many of the private sector sites I've worked on), the sites sometimes get compartmentalized by the group or department responsible for that area of the business (e.g., the Office of Management and Budget is responsible for the management and budget pages of the Website). This often leads to a highly inconsistent site because there are so many different levels of experience and expertise working on the site. I've found that people also get very defensive about their writing (it's the "everyone's a writer" syndrome). They tend to write in long-winded flowery prose, or they are so terse as to be incoherent to all but those who are intimately familiar with the subject.
>
> The writing process is also subject to so many levels of approval that what you end up with looks nothing like what you started with. Imagine if everything you wrote went through a review by at least 12 different people (90 percent of whom are not writers or editors by trade).

You can read *The Cluetrain Manifesto: The End of Business as Usual* at <http://www.cluetrain.com>. It's a thought-provoking challenge to everyone who wants to make money on the Web.

Trying to set guidelines and standards for content (even very broad standards) often leads to a backlash since different agencies and departments are very territorial and not about to give up what they see as their right to control "their section of the site." Most view my group more as an Internet service provider than as the site's administrators and developers.

In other words, writing for a government Website is often an exercise in futility.

While Martin's view reflects a real situation, don't let it discourage you. If you are writing for a corporate Website, private or public, you may need to be a very good politician and a patient advocate. If you must explain the principles of good Webwriting to groups who are technically naïve or organizationally at odds with one another, then follow the three Webwriting principles mentioned in Chapter 2 when you make your case for good, consistent writing on the site: Give your group the orientation it needs about the Web; give it information it can use; and give it reasons to act in what it clearly understands are its own best interests. Whether they're marketing government statistics, college courses, party memberships, or shareware, your colleagues need to understand how marketing works on the Web — and you're the person who has to sell them on that concept.

This doesn't mean sermonizing to these groups during committee meetings. More likely it will mean presenting them with a basic concept and approach toward the creation of the Website that they can understand, that harmonizes with the group's communication style in other media, and that gives them the kind of jolt that visitors to the site should get.

Components of Corporate Web Sites

Mission statements

Placing a mission statement on a Website may pose a challenge to Webwriters. Nancy Eaton, editor of the Webzine *Retro,* warns against "passive voice, formal tone, hype," and other language abuses; mission statements are all too often rich in examples of such abuses. What's more, using an overly formal tone or passive voice may mean your mission statement does not accurately represent your organization.

So if you're going to put your organization's mission statement on your site (and you should), maybe you'd better hold a few meetings to examine it first. A good principle for expressing a mission statement is WISIWYG — What I say is what you get. In other words, if you can't deliver it, don't promise it in your mission statement or anywhere else on your site. And if all you promise is jargon and hype, your readers will see that and surf on to a more welcoming site.

Your mission statement should be on a page of its own, with links to other important pages on the site. You can give readers a chance to respond to the statement by including an email link on the mission-statement page — but make it a link to the company president or the chair of the board of directors, not to the company Webmaster. That way, readers will understand that their opinions are going straight to the decision-makers.

Policies

Corporate policies can also pose problems on Websites. Many organizations deal with the public under the terms of very specific policies (sometimes self-created, sometimes imposed by law). They tend to take those policies for granted, as the "fine print" that no one pays attention to.

Pay attention to your group's policies. If you're a retailer with an iron-clad need for a returned-goods policy that won't bankrupt you, make sure that policy is up on your Website, in large print, so you can refer your customers to it if they haven't found it on their own. If you are creating the Website for a school board with a specific policy about handling parent complaints, that policy should be up in plain English on your school district's Website.

Your group's policies are, in a sense, a contract with the people you serve. Your customers need to know how best to deal with you, and you need to define exactly what you can and can't do for them. And you have to define this in terms that appeal to the reader's own self-interest. It's not an easy job, but do it right and you will enjoy better interaction with your customers.

Archives

You don't have to persuade your group to abandon everything it knows about communicating with the public through other media. Much of your Website's content can be plain old print text stored on your site in the form of archives.

Annual and special reports, news releases, and texts of executives' speeches can all go straight into your site's archives, whether as text files or as pdf (portable document format) files that retain their original word-processed format. You may be able to add value to these archives by creating links within the text to other resources on your site or on the Web, but even as simple archives, such documents are a valuable service to your readers.

Other documents may work either as straight archives or as hypertext. For example, a collective agreement could appear as a straight scrolling text, or as a sequence of chunks, each just a few paragraphs long. Links on such short pages could show readers how one part of the agreement influences another. Policies can be organized similarly, perhaps with links to relevant laws or to comparable policies in other organizations.

For more information on corporate Website development, see *Winning Web Sites*, another book in the Self-Counsel Series.

7
PERSONAL PAGES, RÉSUMÉS, AND SELF-MARKETING

Personal Pages

A personal Web page may have several purposes, from displaying your hobbies and interests to self-marketing. At its basic level, a personal Web page is a lot like an introductory conversation in which you're telling your new acquaintances what you want them to know about you. But what you mostly want to tell them is how you can be helpful to them in some area of shared interest.

Such a conversation usually starts with an attempt to find common ground: similar occupations, hobbies, politics, and interests. Once we're on that common ground, we often give advice: "You're going to Italy? Are you visiting Capri? Super! Well, be sure to stay at the Villa Verdi — excellent rooms, great food, very reasonable. Here's the address."

In other words, we don't just brag about our world travels or our collection of 78 RPM jazz recordings. We cement our friendship by giving our new friends some useful and interesting advice.

Bear in mind that almost no one is going to find your site by typing your name into a search engine. More likely they're looking for information on Italy or on Bix Beiderbecke, and the search will bring up your page because words like "Italy" or "Beiderbecke" appear on it. If all you've got is "I loved visiting Italy in 1991," or "Beiderbecke is great," your visitors will be gone in a flash.

But if you provide useful information, visitors will stick around: addresses and descriptions of some good Italian hotels or an annotated Beiderbecke discography will make their visit worthwhile. If you promise updated or expanded information, your visitors will bookmark your site and return to it. Better yet, they may get in touch with you by email to share their interests — and now your visitors are also friends who can help you pursue your common interests.

As well as being useful, your personal page should be easy to use. That usually means containing graphics that are small or not containing any graphics at all. A huge graphic may take forever to download, and visitors may not stick around just to see a snapshot of the family dog. Ideally, the front page is a table of contents leading to other pages, such as travel tips, hobbies, and a personal résumé. Your subjects should be clear; if your interest is strictly in jazz, the subject should be Jazz, not Music. If you have room, a short blurb can help:

Jazz Interests: Beiderbecke rules!

Travel Advice: Italy especially

While your personal page ought to express your personality, remember that its purpose is to offer a service of some kind, not to let you indulge yourself. This is especially true when you're promoting yourself or your organization for the professional services you offer.

The services you offer may include links to similar sites — the Italian Tourism Office, for example — but it's a good idea to place those links deep inside your own site. Let your visitors first learn about Capri from you; then, if they want more information, they can surf away to another site.

Beyond the Print Résumé

Just as you should make your personal Website useful to your readers, your online résumé should make you appear useful to potential employers. But this is a little trickier than just listing your favorite jazz musicians and Italian hotels.

For one thing, a lot of people are ahead of you. One particular Website, the Monster Board, has an estimated 300,000 résumés in its data base; its Canadian affiliate reportedly gathered 45,000 résumés in its first year of operation. The Monster Board claims that 80,000 job seekers come to its site each day. And it's only one of hundreds of sites that try to match up jobs and people. If your résumé is going to stand out, you'll need to do things better than most people.

The Monster Board is at <http://www.monster.com>. The Canadian Monster Board is at <http://www.monster.ca>.

Make a good first impression

When we write Web documents, we bring some habits from print. They don't always apply in hypertext, however, and this is especially true of the résumé. The print-on-paper résumé works on the principle of the good first impression. First we like (or dislike) the general look of the résumé. Then we gain our impression of the person from the first things we learn about him or her — from what's at the top of the résumé. We carry on through the résumé paying most attention to whatever section comes first, and to whatever is at the top of a given section.

If you put your education at the top of the résumé we assume that your education is your strongest selling point. If you put your most recent education at the top of the section, we assume that's your most relevant training. That's why print résumés work in reverse chronological order: they're trying to show employers that the applicant has strong, recent experience or training in areas that the employer thinks are important.

If you follow this principle too closely, of course, you may run into trouble. Suppose you want a job as a tour guide, and you have lots of experience, but since last summer you've kept yourself alive with a series of joe jobs in the local mall. In strict reverse chronology, your work-experience section makes you look like a qualified salesperson, not a tour guide.

The answer in a print résumé is to create a special category, Tour Guide Experience, and another category for the mall jobs, Other Experience (details available on request), which you put far down the résumé where it won't draw much attention.

So if you're using the Web to market yourself, how do you organize your electronic résumé?

You have a couple of options. You could make it a long, scrolling document, or a stack of short pages linked to a front page. The scrolling document is technically easier to create, since it's just one file and it keeps everything unified. When your readers open your résumé, the first thing they see is whatever you think is your strongest qualification. They can then scroll down through the rest of the résumé, learning more about you.

If you create a stack of pages, the front page is really just a table of contents, a set of buttons that link to an education page or a work-experience page. This gives your readers the chance to decide for themselves what's most important about you from their point of view: your recent training, your work experience, or your specific work skills.

Maybe, however, the employer has an old modem, and skipping from page to page is painfully slow. That could be annoying. An alternative could be to create a set of links at the top of a single page: education, tour guide experience, volunteer experience, work skills. The employer can then rappel down your page, hopping straight to the section of most interest — with a button in each section that will lead back to the top of the page for another hop.

Choose the organizational structure you think will create the least trouble for employers. Within each section, display your information as you would in a regular print résumé: for example, job title, summary of duties, perhaps the name of your supervisor and your reason for leaving.

What if your school or previous employer has a Web page — do you provide a link? If you do, you're probably wiser putting such links on a separate page or at the bottom of the résumé. Otherwise you risk distracting your readers by inviting them to jump to a site that's really not relevant to your purposes. This résumé is about you, after all, not about your last employer or the college you attended 12 years ago.

Surprise: Redefine yourself as different

One hazard for all job-seekers is presenting the right mix of reassurance and surprise to potential employers. Employers are anxious souls, always worrying that they'll hire the wrong person. That's one reason why they like to see a very traditionally designed résumé; the design itself says you're a traditional, reliable kind of person. Of course, when everyone's doing traditional design, you look like everyone else and the employer may recover from anxiety only to find you boring.

In print, you can set yourself apart from the herd by presenting an unusual layout, by adopting a different tone (maybe very informal), or even by using a distinctive font or pale-lavender paper. On the Web you can do the same things, but they may backfire. Unusual layouts may just look awkward on your employer's particular browser and platform. A page designed for a big monitor may look terrible on a small one. A knockout special effect (or even access to the page itself) doesn't even happen if the reader lacks a particular plug-in. The background color you chose so carefully may never show up if the reader's browser has the wrong settings, and your classy font may not show up either if your reader doesn't have the font on his or her computer.

You will notice that I've discussed only problems with display; on the Web, the reader largely decides how a page will display. But whether your text appears in 12-point Times Roman or 14-point Palatino, the content will remain the same. So it's in content that you'll be able to set yourself apart from your competitors by giving the employer a pleasant surprise or two.

Plain English will be the first such surprise. Many job-seekers on the Web are technical and scientific workers, businesspeople, and bureaucrats. They're used to writing a thick, kludgy, verbose English even though they say they hate such a style in their colleagues' writing. Where such a technical style is critical to accuracy, it's perfectly OK to use it — but don't use a technical style when you don't need to.

Plain English gives you several advantages in presenting your qualifications in a Web-based résumé:

(a) *Pleasure.* Readers can actually understand, at once, what you're telling them. Most will find this a welcome change, and since good writers of plain English are scarce, you've added yet another qualification to your skill list.

(b) *Speed.* Remember that the monitor slows down reading speed. Plain English, concisely written, will help readers get the message faster.

(c) *Nonverbal confidence message.* Plain English tells the reader you're confident in yourself and your understanding of the field in which you work. You're not trying to impress by using business English or bureaucratese or technobabble. Sure, you know those dialects, and you can use them when necessary, but you're not talking shop in your résumé — you're making a sales pitch for yourself. The more people who understand you, the more potential employers you have.

Your Web résumé has other nonverbal messages. These messages are critical for the way they support or undercut your verbal message.

Suppose you're presenting yourself in your text as a capable Web designer — but your own site organization is clumsy and confusing, with unappealing graphics and spelling errors in the text. Which message will your readers believe, the verbal (what you say on your site) or the nonverbal (how you say it)? The nonverbal, of course. If you need more proof, look at almost any Web designer's page and ask yourself: Would I hire this person to design my own page?

Or suppose you create an exquisitely advanced site, full of clever technical surprises in graphics, audio, and video. The nonverbal message in such a site is: Only the equally technologically advanced, those with all the plug-ins and a really fast Internet connection, need to visit here. That may make some employers feel right at home. Or it may not. The most sophisticated Web users understand that you don't do something just because it's technically doable, but rather because it's the simplest, most effective way to convey a message. When such sophisticated users are the kind of employers you want to reach, less really is more.

Probably the best surprise you can offer a potential employer is the nonverbal message that you know your area of expertise, you enjoy using that expertise, and you're not trying to impress anyone with irrelevant information. If you judge your online résumé by the three principles of good Webwriting (i.e., Orientation, Information, and Action), and it passes, chances are your potential employer will be very pleasantly surprised indeed.

Create a portfolio on your site

Many job seekers turn up for a hiring interview with a portfolio that demonstrates their skills: reports written for previous employers, copies of ads they've written or designed, photos they've taken, letters of commendation, and awards. These can be an effective way of showing, not just telling, potential employers what you can do for them.

Your Website can serve as a portfolio that employers can consult even before they call you in for an interview. Consider some of the items you could include in your portfolio:

- Reference letters

- Awards

- Evaluations by previous employers

- Degrees and certificates

- Course descriptions or outlines (both for courses you've taken and courses you've taught)

- Writing samples: technical reports, business plans, proposals, ad copy, news releases, novels in progress, poetry

- Graphics samples: photos, video clips, line art

- News stories (whether by you or about you)

- Links to organizations or individuals

Some of these elements need careful thought. For example, do you want to include a scanned graphic of your college degree, or of an award you won as a freelance writer? Maybe, but from the employer's point of view, will the jolt of seeing the graphic be worth the wait? Are the writing samples really relevant to the job you're seeking, or just the kind of thing you enjoy doing for yourself?

If you provide an email link to a reference or previous employer, has that person given you permission to do so? After all, you're asking the person to go to the trouble of replying to queries about you — maybe a lot of them — and it's simple courtesy to check first to see if that's OK.

Less Is More
Remember the idea of minimalism discussed in Chapter 2: Webwriting should be just long enough to do the intended job and no longer. Don't include too many writing samples, or samples unrelated to the kind of writing you'd do for the job in question.

Provide useful services

Your Web résumé should supply a benefit to potential employers even if they don't hire you. Maybe you're an accountant who's helped design a new spreadsheet; let your readers link to a demo version of the spreadsheet. Or, as a safety consultant, you developed emergency procedures for open-pit mines; archive your guidelines in easily downloadable form. You were a cook in a local steakhouse? Give us a great barbecue sauce recipe. (In all these examples, I assume you own the rights to what you're offering!)

If you've got the skills to be worth hiring, you know something useful that you can give away. By doing so you build goodwill and likely reach potential employers who will never see your Website — but they may well see a copy of your spreadsheet or guidelines or recipe that has been forwarded to them by someone else, and get in touch with you because they like what they've seen of your work. If they're really sensitive to the culture of the Web, they'll also recognize that out on the electronic frontier, pioneers lend a hand to one another — and since you've lent them a hand, they may be able to return the favor.

Make response easy

For Jakob Nielsen's convincingly critical view of frames, see <http://www.useit.com/alertbox/9612.html>.

Your readers may well hop from page to page in your résumé. If they like what they see, getting in touch with you should be as easy as you can make it. This is really a design question inspired by the "you" attitude. For example, each page should have a link titled something like Email Me. Click on it, and an email form pops up, pre-addressed to you. Or each page could include your name and address plus telephone number(s) and email address. That way, readers always know how to reach you. (You could create a frame with such data that is visible everywhere on your site, but I side with Jakob Nielsen on this issue: Frames are a classic example of doing something because you can, not because it's really helpful or useful to the user.)

Ease of access, by the way, sends another nonverbal message: I'm thinking of your needs and making life as easy as I can for you.

Another thoughtful touch: In addition to your online résumé, whether scrolling or chunked, provide a version that employers can print out for themselves for easy reference. Keep it simple and short — not more than three pages and preferably one or two. Normally such a version would not contain elaborate formatting, links, or other Web-dependent effects: just words and white space, laid out for easy readability.

Use Your Personal Site Pro-Actively

Don't just put your personal site up on the World Wide Web and sit back waiting for employer email to start pouring in. Most employers prefer hiring through traditional channels: the hidden job market of personal connections first, and then public recruiting and shortlisting if no one suitable turns up in the hidden job market. An employer who goes out searching for employees on the Web is probably desperate for some rare skill set — and such an employer isn't necessarily going to have the Web-search skills that will turn up your site.

So make your site a part of your own active job search. When you apply for a publicly advertised job, by all means give your site's URL. If you go "prospecting" (interviewing potential employers for information, not for a specific job), invite the person you're prospecting to take a look at your site while you're there. If it's a Web-related job you're after, the prospect presumably knows enough about the medium to be impressed with what you've got — and to offer useful advice on your errors and omissions. Don't be embarrassed, be grateful! Such critiques can only make your site — and your qualifications — look better.

One final point: Very few people ever get a job through their résumé alone. As I suggested at the start of this chapter, all your résumé can really do is create a good first impression that encourages potential employers to learn more about you in a face-to-face interview. If your online résumé gets you that interview, it's done all it can.

Case Study 3: An Online Résumé

Freelancin' Babes International

Karen Solomon's Website is located at <http://www.dnai.com/~ksolomon/>.

Karen Solomon is a freelance writer with a lot of Web experience. She uses her personal Website to present her skills and experience, and also her attitude. She kindly agreed to let me use parts of her site as a case study. Here's the text of the front page of her site:

> Karen Solomon, Web Writer
>
> Freelancin' Babes International
>
> San Francisco, California
>
> (415) 242-9553
>
> I can write 1,000 words worth more than any stoopid picture.
>
> Omniscience, omnipresence, and ubiquity are my specialties.
>
> In fact, I know you want to hire me.
>
> Strunk and White are my idols. I am Queen of the tight phrase, the trig one-liner, and the terse summation. Check out my fancy footwork below.
>
> Reviews Features Experience Resume Links Contact

Comment:

Solomon immediately establishes an ironic personal style with her "Freelancin' Babes International" corporate name. She builds on the irony with "stoopid," and with the deliberate emphasis on Latinate diction: "omniscience, omnipresence, and ubiquity." She invokes Strunk and White (*The Elements of Style*), complete with a link to the Website of that classic guide, knowing perfectly well that Strunk and White would have taken issue with some of her word choices and the tone they create. Irony continues with "Queen of the tight phrase, the trig one-liner" (trig being an archaic word for tidy), and with the sudden shift to a casual tone: "Check out my fancy footwork below," followed by links to other pages on her site.

The overall impact is amusing and engaging — providing a jolt that makes us want to learn more about this writer with the offbeat sense of humor. Irony, however, can be dangerous; it pays us the compliment of assuming we're able to see the real message hiding beneath the surface of the text, but we may not be as perceptive as we should be. Some readers might see the dissonance between verbal and nonverbal messages, but simply assume the writer isn't very serious about herself or her skills — and, therefore, won't be very serious about her clients' needs either.

Still, the offbeat approach tempts us to look further. Here's a page of excerpts from Website reviews that Karen has written:

Enjoy excerpts from Lycos Press'

"Most Popular Web Sites:

The Best of the Net From A2z"

Extropy Institute

Study the spearhead of the transhumanist movement. Extropy explores how you can live, behave, and act toward your fullest, ultrahuman potential. Peruse current and back issues of their monthly magazine, plus long-standing articles such as, "Uploading Yourself" and "Robotics" t\hat reveal and criticize humanity's relationship with Artificial Intelligence and a cyber/electronic culture.

The Western Canon

The definitive what's what and who's who of every author, -ism, and -ist throughout the history of literature. An excellent quick reference and brief summary guide searchable by author, subject, or time period that illuminates such mysteries as the difference between Romanticism and Harlequins, Modern and Postmodern, Virgil and Vergil. You can also join the mailing list or vote for your favorite intellectual superhero.

Literary Kicks

View the hep cat cool daddy-o biographies of famous beat artists and writers such as Ginsberg, Kerauac, Cassady, and Burroughs. Learn more about the Beat Generation, their writing, and their relationship to modern popular and electronic culture. Also, keep abreast of the latest Beat News, including the Ginsberg tribute page.

Maya Angelou

This lovely group effort from the University of Texas is a tribute to the former Poet Laureate. In addition to listing all of Angelou's books, there are numerous links to her poems online, including a sound byte of her reading her work. If you have more time to download large files, take a look at the video clip of her reading at the Million Man March. Also includes some literary criticism.

Comment:

The irony becomes a problem in some of these thumbnail reviews. Does Solomon take terms like "ultrahuman potential" seriously, or is she poking fun at some 1990s version of 1970s psychobabble? "Literary superhero" uses a term from the pop culture of comic books; is she trivializing the authors that the site is celebrating? Is "hep cat cool daddy-o" an affectionate use of dated slang, or a put-down of yesterday's literary giants? (Misspelling Kerouac's name is unfortunate.) It's helpful to know that the Maya Angelou clip is a large file that may take some time to download.

Finally, let's look at Solomon's actual résumé:

Karen Solomon

Web Writer

San Francisco, California

(415) 242-9553

EXPERIENCE

KnowledgeWeb.com

July, 1997 - present

Writer

Crafting syndicated daily and monthly horoscopes for

Netstrology, Astrology.Net, Elle, and GoodCompany amongst others.

Composed an astrological compatibility data base.

Other projects include some marketing research and site interface design.

Contact: Kelli Fox, Founder/Publisher

CNET: The Computer Network

On and Off, March, 1997 - present

Freelance Website Reviewer

Cataloging and reviewing topical sites for the Web directory,

Snap.com.

Contact: Paul Wood, Speciality Services

Lycos Press

May, 1997

A2z Project Editor and Writer

Writing reviews for their massive print publication,

Most Popular Web Sites: The Best of The Net From A2z

Contact: Kathleen McFadden, Revisions Editor

InfoMation Publishing Corporation/The Password

March, 1997 - March, 1998

Freelance Specialty Paper Editor

Shaping and editing Web content to compose informative and comprehensive online magazines. Exercised my Web savvy and well-honed research skills.

Contact: John Palace, Editorial Director or Christopher Cummings, Content Editor

Tokushima Prefecture, Japan

July, 1995 - July, 1996

Assistant English Teacher

As well as teaching English, I wrote numerous articles for local publication, assisted in translation and editing, and promoted community cultural exchange.

COMPUTER EXPERIENCE

Proficient in both Macintosh and PC platforms, Word, Word Perfect, Aldus Pagemaker, FileMaker Pro, Microsoft Access, Quark Xpress, PowerPoint, Netscape, Internet Explorer, HTML, Internet tools (Telnet, FTP, etc.), some Unix.

Web Site, Reviews, Features, Tech Reviews, Resume, Links, Contact

Comment:

Karen Solomon could take much more advantage of hypertext here. She lists her work background in standard reverse-chronological order, with no other organizing principle. Most of the work is Web-related, but not all; the English teaching in Japan, while interesting, also seems slightly incongruous at the end of all the Web experience.

Another approach might be to present herself as having a broad range of writing and Web skills, listed with the most critical ones displayed at the top of the résumé, regardless of when she gained them. The Web reviewing, for example, must demand a keen and analytical insight suitable for many different kinds of Webwriting. If she started with that, and listed the astrology writing as just one kind of writing she's capable of, her expertise would look deeper and wider. Teaching and writing in Japan must have required good cross-cultural communication skills — which could be very valuable as more Websites become multilingual and multicultural.

With so many freelance jobs based on short-term contracts, your most recent job may be the least typical, or the worst in displaying your most important skills and talents. So a strictly chronological résumé may typecast you into the wrong role, while a résumé organized by skills (whenever and wherever obtained) can keep those skills uppermost in the minds of potential employers.

8
ADVOCACY AND MARKETING ON THE WEB

Information is telling people how many motels there are in Chesterton; advocacy is persuading people to visit Chesterton because it will meet their needs; and marketing is persuading people to make a reservation at one of those motels. Many principles of advocacy and marketing in other media are the same on the Web. If your Website's purpose is to promote a point of view or to sell an item or service, it's more likely to succeed if you keep in mind some basic principles of persuasion.

Semantics and Register

Many words have complex connotations. That is, they don't just refer to a particular thing or action or idea; they convey some kind of emotional aura as well. A restaurant may be a "fast-food joint" or a "bistro" — both offer quick service, but a bistro sounds classier. "Good eats" promises something different from "an elegant dining experience."

Semantics is the study of such meanings, and semanticists like to distinguish between "purr words" and "snarl words" — words whose connotations are either positive (at least to the speaker or writer) or negative. Such words may refer to the same thing, but carry very different meanings: "Certified General Accountant" and "bean counter," for example, or "vintage automobile" and "beater," or "educator" and "pedant." In effect, purr words and snarl words convey our attitude toward whatever we're discussing.

As a persuasive Webwriter, then, you should be aware of how your readers will respond to the words you choose. You should also consider the register to adopt in your text. Register involves choosing words that reflect your understanding of the social situation and how the people involved see one another. When you write to a stranger, you address her as "Dear Ms. Robinson." That's the register of formal business writing, and Ms. Robinson accepts this term as a courtesy one stranger pays to another. Once you've become friends, you can write "Dear Helen," in a much less formal register. And what happens when you write "Dearest," or "Sweetest Helen"? Suddenly you're in a much more intimate register, and you'd better hope she doesn't write back, "Dear Mr. Smith"!

Register doesn't just convey the proper manners for the occasion. It can also determine the content of your message. When the president addresses the combined House and Senate, he doesn't say: "Folks, I am really ticked off about the way my political opponents are pulling my chain on the defense budget." He says: "Thank you, Mr. Speaker. My fellow Americans…" As a rule, the more people you're addressing at once, the more formal and abstract your message is likely to be. The fewer people you're addressing, the more informal and personal you can be.

What does that mean for you as a Webwriter? Maybe thousands of people will visit your site; should you adopt an elevated "public" register, as if you were addressing a huge political rally? Or, since each reader arrives at your site as an individual, can you adopt an intimate personal register?

That depends to some extent on the nature of your site. If its purpose is to represent a "serious" organization — a bank, an environmental activist group, a political party's local branch — then the register should be serious also. Such organizations exist because of people's hopes and anxieties, and no one wants to be even more anxious about the security of their savings or the direction their country is taking because of reading text with an inappropriate tone on an organization's Website. This is why bankers and politicians tend to dress conservatively, unless they're trying for a "plain folks" image. They also speak conservatively and would expect cautious, correct language on their organization's Website.

If the organization's purpose is fun, then the register ought to convey that. The Website for a company that makes squirt guns or that markets backpacks to young world travelers is obviously going to be relaxed and lighthearted. It can afford to use slang or incorrect English, or even to exclude some people by using in-group terms.

Whether serious or fun, your site is trying to assure your readers that you speak their language, and that they can, therefore, trust you. If your use of semantics and register makes them feel like outsiders, they will be skeptical of your claims.

Three Elements of Persuasion

When you're writing to persuade your readers, you may have varied goals. If you want to reinforce readers' existing beliefs and values (also known as preaching to the choir), you have an easy job. We're always eager to hear that we're right. Changing your readers' beliefs is harder, and requires trust from your readers that you are concerned with their best interests. Hardest of all is getting people to act, even when you've been telling them they're right.

Bear in mind the major elements of good Webwriting: Orientation, Information, and Action. If you make it easy for your readers to respond, they will get in the habit of acting. Short, powerful chunks of text can trigger strong emotions and willingness to act. In some ways, the Web poses an ethical problem for the persuader: It's not suitable for careful, linear, logical argument, and it's excellent for jolt-rich slogans, captions, and unsupported assertions. Yet manipulating readers by appealing to their fears and insecurities is deeply disrespectful. If you're attempting to persuade your readers, it should be on the basis of appeals to their intelligence and maturity.

With that in mind, let's look at three aspects of persuasion as they operate on the Web.

Logical argument

Logical argument involves stating a proposition of some kind, along with supporting reasons. The reasons themselves must be supportable. So you might predict that the US population in 2050 will reach 394 million, with 20 million being women aged 80 or more. You could cite the US Bureau of the Census as your support for this argument, and perhaps that would be enough authority for most people. If you think it is not enough for your particular audience, you would also have to describe the Census Bureau's methodology in reaching its prediction. Assuming that the methodology used generally accepted statistical projections (accepted because they've been accurate in the past), you could safely assert that you've made a logical argument for your population forecast.

Emotional appeal

By invoking ideas and images that stir our readers' feelings, we can gain interest that logical argument alone may not achieve. In some cases, we may not even care about the logic in an argument until something has dragged us emotionally into a confrontation with the issue. Only then will some people seek the logical argument to back up their strong feelings.

Again, the online advocate should be careful to avoid exploiting readers' anxieties. Appeals to emotion should be positive (invoking love, trust, friendship, or noble qualities like courage and honesty), rather than appealing to fear, hatred, and contempt.

This doesn't mean a positive emotional appeal is automatically a good argument. Love and courage are admirable, but they may serve detestable causes. The Aryan Nations assert on their Website that their policies are motivated by love, especially love for white children. Stormfront, another white-supremacist site, hails the "courageous men and women" struggling to defend "White Western Culture."

Unless you support a position because of strong emotions you don't want to examine, you probably came to your position by learning particular facts. These facts, in the context of your particular values, caused you to adopt the position you're now advocating. You may, therefore, find that facts, not loaded language, can inspire similar emotions in your readers.

Credibility

Using your readers' language and registers they're comfortable with can strongly enhance your credibility. But you also need to demonstrate some kind of shared interest between yourself and your readers, and convey sincerity through your tone and evident desire to help readers who visit your site. You should also have acceptable credentials — direct personal experience, specialized training, or at least a selection of respected and recognized authorities who can back up your assertions.

Relying on the "you" attitude can help your credibility by putting your arguments in terms of the reader's interest rather than your own. In its crudest form, this gives us the "crazy" retailer who's giving you a bargain that will probably bankrupt him or her. But if you can establish that you serve your own interests best by serving your reader's interests, you further enhance reader trust in you.

Some unscrupulous persuaders like to "stack the deck" by presenting only the information that makes them look good. A more effective way to establish credibility is to raise opposing arguments as serious objections — and then refute them. A frequently asked questions (FAQs) page — a page where such questions are cited and then answered — can also be an effective way to state your readers' reservations and show how you can demolish them.

A good example of writing that establishes credibility is the essay "Rush Limbaugh on Global Warming," by Charles Ess, professor of philosophy and religion at Drury College in Springfield, Missouri. It's available at <http://www.drury.edu/faculty/Ess/Limbaugh.html>.

Constructing Persuasive Webtext

Maybe you just want readers to accept your argument passively, but more likely you want them to act on it — to buy the product, vote for the candidate, protest the outrage. As we've seen, Webtext doesn't lend itself to long, cumulative, reasoned argument, and it doesn't have the emotionally overwhelming impact of a wide-screen movie with stereo sound. Given its limits, the medium can still stir readers to respond to your message if you remember the principles of Orientation, Information, and Action.

Orientation

Your readers want to know where they are when they arrive at your site, and they also want to know where they stand in relation to you. If they feel you're on their side, they'll welcome your message more easily. You can establish rapport with readers if you —

- *Show you understand your readers' concerns.* You can often do this by identifying something that your readers will recognize as a problem. The problem could be an oppressive government or the difficulty of saving money for a holiday.

- *Offer something that readers will agree with.* A generalization or striking slogan can make readers think they've found a kindred soul. It doesn't have to be a cliché, but it should state, as Alexander Pope observed, "what oft was thought, but ne'er so well expressed."

- *Ask for help.* Readers have the power to decide, to choose, to buy, to join, and you want readers to be aware of that power.

- *Suggest a benefit.* If your readers agree that a problem exists, offer a solution they will find beneficial: greater peace of mind, a clear conscience, a new experience.

Information

Your readers will want details of the facts backing up your argument. By providing further information, your argument becomes more legitimate and appealing to your readers. Try the following —

- Explain the benefit in some detail, using facts and figures if necessary.

- Surprise your reader with a new fact or perspective on a familiar subject; a reader with a new idea or understanding is open to persuasion. We trust people who are on our wavelength but ahead of us in understanding the issue.

- Discuss objections or drawbacks calmly, then rebut them and focus on positive arguments. Most of us have been fooled often enough to be suspicious of offers and arguments that are literally too good to be true, so readers will be suspicious even when they want to believe you.

Action

Make sure your argument ends with a strong call to action. The following tips can help encourage readers to take whatever action you would like them to:

- Show how action can solve the problem you've described. You may give examples of earlier actions that got the desired results (Last year's campaign paid for clean water supplies for six villages) or unhappy results based on failure to act (Sixty-two children in the region died of cholera last year because of contaminated water).

- Make the desired action clear and easy. A complicated or time-consuming response will make your reader hesitate. (Just type in your name and email address. Simply click on the Yes or No button to register your opinion instantly! Test your understanding with this quick quiz.)

- Stress the benefit of responding quickly. Whether you're selling Alaska cruises or party memberships, delay can be fatal to your campaign. If appropriate, set a deadline: Email us by September 15 and get a free consultation ($250 value).

What's a Legitimate Appeal? What's Not?

You can legitimately appeal to —

- Recognized authorities — people or organizations generally accepted as expert and reliable in their field

- Scientific experiment and observation, producing results that others can duplicate

- Logical deduction or extrapolation from established facts

- Readers' emotions, but only when combined with other legitimate appeals

You're on shaky ground if you appeal to —

- Anecdotal evidence (My cousin was abducted by aliens)

- Celebrity (Charlton Heston opposes gun registration)

- Outside authorities trading on irrelevant expertise (Joe Doakes, a nuclear physicist, says UFOs exist)

You're out of bounds if you appeal to —

- Logical fallacies — mistakes in argument that sound logical but aren't (see Stephen's Guide to the Logical Fallacies Website at <http://www.intrepidsoftware.com/fallacy/welcome.htm>)

- Hasty generalizations (I lost a fortune in a Canadian casino; Canadians are a bunch of crooks)

- Wishful thinking (This stock is sure to go up)

- Readers' prejudices (Are you sick of the disaster in the public schools?)

- False authorities (The Protocols of the Elders of Zion prove the Jews want to take over the world — this argument is still made by anti-Semites, though the "Protocols" were long ago proven to be a forgery of the Tsarist secret police who plagiarized them from a French satire on Napoleon III published in the 1860s)

Case Study 4: Persuasive Argument on the Web

An Argument for Equal Opportunity

Lisa Schmitt, a technical writer, had the following essay on her Website in the autumn of 1998 and kindly volunteered it as a case study for this book. Let's consider how she makes her arguments and how she might revise the essay to make it a more persuasive Web document.

This essay used to be available on the Web at <http://www.angelfire.com/ar/wordpower/nightmare.html> but unfortunately it is no longer posted.

I've noticed an odd phenomenon in the past dozen or so years. In spite of the ever-increasing litigation faced by business and industry, some people just don't get the message. In far too many businesses the "good ol' boy" network still seems to believe that it's above having to clean up its act to remain in the business world.

Some of the places I've witnessed the problems, I've been on the receiving end of the comments or actions. In others, I have witnessed actions tolerated by co-workers and friends that are blatant violations of EOC regulations, among others. How is it that, in spite of the readily available means to deal with them, these cretins are allowed to continue?

At one employer where I worked, the owner used vicious personal attacks to deal with his employees when he had a disagreement with them. Name calling, belittling, and harassment were not below his level. Even with a turnover rate exceeding 50 percent some years, he continues to go about his business. Rather than addressing the issue that is affecting the employees' performance, he attacks personal appearance, lineage, race, religion, sexual orientation, and about every other protected area imaginable.

In another situation, we dealt with a group of four men who ran the operation. These men would "cover" each other and their cronies, but God help those who would cross them. Theft, destruction of property, blatant violations of sexual harassment policies, and severe infringement on rights protected by EOC and other regulations have all been swept under the rug. One person, in particular, had an entire department ready to quit because his harassment and abuse of the people he supervised were so egregious.

Acts that affected the lives of two of my friends, as well as their families, were carried out by another company. One of those involved a pregnant female being required to participate in an activity that was hazardous. An accident resulted in the loss of her child, a lovely little girl. The company accepted no responsibility. Rather, they required her to return to work, against the advice of her doctor, or face the immediate loss of her job.

The other, a black male, was working as a contractor at the same company. Of all the people there, he was one of the most reliable. He was seldom seen talking to co-workers during work hours, didn't come in late or leave early. He was someone I would be proud to have working for me today. He was terminated from the job after being told the company was over budget for contractors. Funny thing, though, less than 72 hours later, a new contractor was in there. Racially motivated? Who knows?

In all the above cases, no legal action has been taken to address the issues they raise. I realize that without being called on to account for their actions, people will not be motivated to change. Unfortunately, when those who are creating the problems are in a position to effectively end your career, not just the current job, how do you find people strong enough, or willing enough, to risk everything for the good of others?

I am as guilty as the rest. Being aware of the situations and not aggressively pursuing some resolution, am I secretly condoning them? Or is it fear that the cost of retribution is higher than even I am willing to pay? We'll see. As days go by, I become much stronger and much less willing to accept the status quo. Maybe I will eventually be the one to sound the alarm for the people who are unfortunate enough to still be working with, or for, those tyrants. I sincerely hope that will be the case. *[620 words]*

Comment:

This is a thoughtful and quietly angry essay, and most readers would probably sympathize with Schmitt's point of view. For a persuasive article to be read off the monitor, however, it's probably a bit long and in some ways might be unclear to many readers. EOC, for example, is an unexplained acronym. Most Americans might know it means Equal Opportunity Commission, but many non-Americans visiting the site would be baffled by it. Schmitt draws on personal experience, which can be very effective (we tend to believe word-of-mouth advertising when we think about buying a car, for example). But we might also suspect that her cases are mere anecdotal evidence, not the signs of a general problem. The essay is also a little slow to establish what it's about. A shorter, more direct version might read something like this:

Why Won't Some Managers Clean Up Their Act?

Too many managers still seem to believe they don't have to clean up their act to remain in the business world.

Blatant expressions of sexism and racism, though they violate the principles of the Equal Opportunity Commission (EOC), are common in the workplace. Sometimes I've been on the receiving end of the comments or actions. In others, I have witnessed actions tolerated by co-workers and friends in spite of the readily available means to deal with them. I suspect that my experience is all too typical.

One of my employers used vicious personal attacks to deal with his employees. Name calling, belittling, and harassment helped create a yearly turnover rate that was sometimes over 50 percent, yet he continues to go about his business.

A Gang of Four

In another case, I dealt with a group of four men who ran the operation. They covered for each other and their cronies, but God help those who would cross them. They concealed theft, destruction of property, blatant violations of sexual harassment policies, and severe infringement on rights protected by EOC. One person, in particular, had his entire department ready to quit because of his harassment and abuse.

She Lost Her Baby

Another case: A pregnant employee was required to take part in a hazardous activity. An accident resulted in the loss of her child, a little girl. The company accepted no responsibility. Rather, it forced her to return to work, against the advice of her doctor, or lose her job.

Over Budget or Just Too Black?

At the same company, a black male was working as a contractor. Of all the people there, he was one of the most reliable. I would be proud to have him working for me today. Yet he was terminated from the job after being told the company was over budget for contractors. Less than 72 hours later, a new contractor was in his place. A racially motivated firing? Who knows?

In all these cases, no one took legal action. Without having to account for their actions, few people are ready to change. Unfortunately, when the "problem bosses" could effectively end your career, not just your current job, you may be reluctant to risk everything for the good of others.

Get Ready to Blow the Whistle

I am as guilty as the rest. Aware of the problems but not aggressively attacking them, am I secretly condoning them? Or do I fear that the cost of retribution is higher than I am willing to pay? We'll see. As days go by, I become much stronger and much less willing to accept the status quo. Maybe I will eventually be the one to sound the alarm for the people who are unfortunate enough to still be working for those tyrants. Or maybe it will be you.

[448 words]

Comment:

Jakob Nielsen tells us that readers scan Webtext rather than read it. So Lisa Schmitt's 600 words could be too long for readers to comfortably read, and the lack of subheads could make it difficult for readers to see where she's going in her argument. By cutting the piece, we can compensate for lower reading speed;

by adding a title and subheads we prepare (and even attract) the reader for the thesis and each point in turn. We could add a sentence about "suspecting" that her experience is a common one, but a stronger point would be some kind of statistical estimate on the number of EOC violations that go unreported.

The essay actually follows the structure suggested by the elements of Orientation, Information, and Action, though the action is still just a hope at the end. As a print article — a column in the local paper, perhaps — it would probably stir a few letters and some complimentary telephone calls ("Let me tell you about my boss!"). But Schmitt might take advantage of the Web's capacity to handle prompt response. She might put a set of links at the bottom of her article, inviting readers to respond either to her, to the EOC itself, or to other organizations concerned about human rights in the workplace. She might also invite readers to cast votes: Is this kind of behavior a problem in your workplace? The results might turn her article into just the kind of whistle-blowing action she dreams of!

Case Study 5: Marketing on the Web

Aunt Jessie's Bed and Breakfast

Persuasion doesn't have to involve big issues like human rights. You can also simply try to attract paying guests to an enjoyable experience. Here's how Alex and Irene Kirkwood were marketing their bed and breakfast in rural British Columbia during the summer of 1998, when my wife and I had the pleasure of staying with them.

While the Kirkwoods' page is fairly text rich, it also contains several graphics (including a portrait of Aunt Jessie), and the paragraphs are short, with plenty of space around them. The "you" attitude is good, but could be even better. The amenities list is inviting and sometimes surprising (an art gallery in a B&B?). It might have more impact as a bulleted list.

Even without a major revision of the text, we can give more impact to the amenities, strengthen an already cordial tone, and convey a little more of the real attractiveness of Aunt Jessie's. Reader response is easy: the site offers both an email address and a toll-free telephone number. The site would require a little scrolling, but not enough to warrant a Top of Page button.

Visit the site of Aunt Jessie's Bed and Breakfast at <http://www.monday.com/auntjessies>

Original version

Aunt Jessie's Bed & Breakfast

On the lakeshore of Bridge Lake, BC

8234 Centennial Road

Bridge Lake, BC V0K 1X0

While travelling through the historic Gold Rush Trail in the Cariboo, stay overnight in our peaceful, modern home on beautiful Bridge Lake. Take a quiet

Revised version

Break your journey through the Cariboo's historic Gold Rush country with an overnight stay in our tranquil, modern home on beautiful Bridge Lake. You can take a stroll around the property or just sit by the lake watching the wildlife.

You have a choice of two guest rooms with double or twin beds (cot available), and a comfortable lounge is at stroll on our property or just sit by the lake and watch the wildlife. In the evening enjoy the sunset or sit by the outdoor fireplace and relax.

We offer in our home, two guest rooms and a lounge, satellite TV, VCR, in each room and lounge. We also have a very relaxing Jacuzzi (robes provided), double or twin beds (cot available). Kitchen and laundry facilities. Come and enjoy our fantastic fishing, wilderness hiking, boating, canoeing, horseback riding (closeby), cross country skiing, snow shoeing, and ice fishing. Swimming is also available.

A full home-cooked breakfast including freshly baked scones, muffins, pancakes or waffles and homemade jams, is served at our unique breakfast bar. Special dietary menus are available. Snacks and additional meals by request. Coffee and tea are complimentary at any reasonable hour.

Children and pets are welcome, however, we do request prior notice. Smoking inside the house is restricted, but we have a designated smoking room (solarium).

your disposal. Satellite TV and VCRs are available in both the lounge and guest rooms. Relax in the jacuzzi (robes provided). Kitchen and laundry facilities are available too.

Outdoors, you can enjoy —

- fantastic fishing (on the ice in winter)

- wilderness hiking

- boating, canoeing, swimming

- nearby horseback riding

- cross country skiing, snow shoeing

In the morning, start your day with a hearty home-cooked breakfast —

- fresh-baked scones

- muffins

- pancakes or waffles with homemade jams

Special dietary menus are available; snacks and additional meals by request. Coffee and tea are complimentary at any reasonable hour.

Please let us know if you're bringing children or pets, so we can make them

Art gallery and gift shop are located in the house for your pleasure. Feel free to browse around.

Click here to see a map.

Visa & M/C are welcome!

"Come and join us for a relaxing and memorable experience!"

Your hosts:

Alex & Irene Kirkwood

(Certified First Aid Instructors)

For reservations: phone or fax: (250) 593-4341 Toll free 1-888-441-0656

Email: jessies@bcinternet.net

welcome. Smokers can enjoy our solarium, while the rest of the house is smoke-free.

Before you leave, enjoy browsing our art gallery and gift shop.

Click Here for a Map of the Bridge Lake District

Visa, MasterCard Welcome!

Your hosts:

Alex & Irene Kirkwood

(Certified First Aid Instructors)

For Reservations — Telephone or Fax (250) 593-4341 Toll free 1-888-441-0656

Email: jessies@bcinternet.net

9
FREQUENTLY ASKED QUESTIONS

The Web is already home to many flourishing genres, from muckraking journalism to erotica to avant-garde fiction. Each of these genres probably deserves a book of its own, and will doubtless get it before long. The theory of such forms of Webwriting will emerge from actual practice as thousands of writers experiment to see what works and what doesn't, right on the Web itself.

While looking forward to the appearance of such books, let's try to deal with some basic questions and point interested readers to the ongoing discussions that are attempting to answer them.

Can I make money as a freelance writer on the Web?

Some can, and many are trying. In some cases, freelancers are simply using the Web as a faster way to pitch story ideas to editors of print-based periodicals. In the mid-1990s, this often worked well because email was still a relative novelty and editors paid more attention to electronic queries. Since then, the flood of queries has caused many editors to ignore electronic queries on principle.

Freelancing for e-zines can make money in some cases; the big e-zines pay for the work they publish, at rates ranging from 20¢ to $1 a word. But it's as tough for the unknown novice to break into Web freelancing as it is to break into print media. Still, resources for freelancers are plentiful.

Here's a list of Websites that are useful to freelance writers, supplied (with comments) by Tara Calishain, author of the excellent book The Official Netscape Guide to Online Research (Ventana Books, 1997):

- Make your first stop Inkspot, my fave-rave spot for writers on the Web. Searchable market listings, paying and nonpaying markets. <http://www.inkspot.com/classifieds/mkt.html>

- The Writer's Place has 271 listings. <http://www.awoc.com/AWOC-Home.cfm>

- Check out the Writers' Guidelines Database. Over 300 publications covered. Beautifully designed; loads in a snap. <http://mav.net/guidelines/>

- The *Write Markets Report* is a print magazine but also has market listings on its site. <http://www.writersmarkets.com/>

- @Writers has a large market list: <http://members.tripod.com/~awriters/markets.htm>

- The Canadian Authors Association has a meta-list of markets. <http://www.islandnet.com/~caa/links/publish.html>

- Another meta-list of markets is available at <http://www.poewar.com/>

- Writers Write has an alphabetical market listing as well as information on tracking your submissions. <http://www.writerswrite.com/paying/>

- The Market List lists markets for science fiction, fantasy, and horror. <http://www.marketlist.com/>

- Spicy Green Iguana lists paying electronic magazines. <http://members.aol.com/mhatv/main.htm>

- *Write Market Webzine* has market news. <http://www.writemarket.com>

- About.com has a freelance writers' site. <http://freelancewrite.about.com/careers/freelancewrite/>

Can I become a regular staff Webwriter?

For many new Webwriters, the environment is both attractive and frustrating. Getting your work on the Web is easy. Getting paid for it is another matter. Even if you do find a serious employer, it's not clear what terms you should ask for, or expect.

Not long ago I interviewed Melanie Dawn, content director for Stratford Internet Technologies — one of Vancouver's hottest, most rapidly growing firms (<http://www.stratfordinternet.com>). Melanie hires writers for Stratford's many projects, so she knows the field very well. I believe her company's requirements and working conditions are typical of most companies seeking Webwriters. Slightly condensed, here's our email conversation:

Q: Recently you told me current contract rates average about $50 to $60 Canadian per hour, while ranging from $30 to $100 depending on experience. What kind of experience makes a difference? Can a new Stratford writer move up the pay scale after a reasonable time?

Melanie: The current contract rates I quoted are listed in the Freelance Editorial Association Fee and Scheduling Guidelines. (<http://www.tiac.net/users/freelanc/fees.html>). We are willing to pay current contract rates to contractors, but obviously the more experienced the writer is with new media, the better the rate will be.

Experience is based on a variety of factors. We include prior experience writing for a specific target market, expertise on a specific subject, previous experience writing for a Web-related audience and so on. The more experience you have writing for new media, the higher the demand will be for your services.

Writers need to be comfortable with the unique demands of the online medium. They need to understand that they are writing for an audience with a very short attention span and a preference for skim reading. Successful writers are able to adapt their writing style accordingly.

Yes, a Stratford writer can move up the pay scale after a reasonable time.

Q: Apart from payment, what are typical contract terms? Is the writer's work strictly fee for service, or are royalties/resale possible? Are your terms typical for the industry?

Melanie: All content written for the company becomes the sole property of Stratford. If content has already been written, we are willing to consider licensing it for some of our large dot-com projects. However, as far as contract terms are considered, this is a matter between the writer and the company at time of signing. Our terms are typical for the industry.

Q: Are Stratford writers generally "subject experts" who pick up Webwriting as they go along, or expert writers who pick up the subject as required?

Melanie: It depends on the project and whether or not their writing style fits the tone of the site. As an example, for Web of Care, a home health-care community developed by Stratford (<http://www.webofcare.com>), we hired content developers with experience writing health-care-related material. We also contracted with qualified doctors and health-care professionals to contribute content.

We then had our in-house editors revise and optimize it for the Web. For a new entertainment destination that we are currently building, targeting the 18-34 market, we are hiring Webwriters who understand both the audience and the Internet.

Q: Do new Webwriters make "newbie" errors, and if so, what are typical errors? What do they most need to unlearn from earlier writing experience?

Melanie: Newbies tend to be wordy. The goal, however, should be getting a lot of information out in the fewest words. New writers also tend to write in a linear fashion, but for the Web you must often write in short snippets to be displayed in different places.

I don't think writers have to completely unlearn their earlier writing experience. It's a matter of having to wrap your head around learning something new and detaching yourself from old patterns. You take elements of what you've learned in the past and incorporate them. It's an evolution.

Q: What's the most useful non-Web experience for a Webwriter to bring to the job?

Melanie: Life experience, creativity, and the ability to be flexible and open-minded! As I said earlier, things are constantly changing, so the Webwriter can't fear change. Things move much too quickly for that. If you fear change, you'll be left behind.

Q: Do your Webwriters need to be local Vancouver-area writers, or can you hire people anywhere in the world? In particular, do you hire Webwriters resident in the US, UK, and Australia? Are their terms different from those for local (or least Canadian) writers?

Melanie: Presently all of our writers are Vancouver-based. However, we are open to residents from other parts of the world. We require a personal interview with all Webwriters, but their work location is not a major factor once a contract has been signed.

As Stratford grows globally, we will have more writers located in different parts of the world. The medium is really designed to enable people to do just that. It creates relationships globally. For Webofcare.com, one of the doctors who contributed to the site was an Australian licensed to work in the US. He was in South Africa while he made his contributions. Again, the terms established are between the writer and Stratford.

Q: Does "Webwriting" also include editing, whether of one's own work or that of others? Or is Web editing a specialized task?

Melanie: Typically a content editor does the Web editing, but our editors have been known to play both roles. We do not have our writers edit their own work.

Q: Can a Webwriter "pitch" Stratford on particular content, or does Stratford simply assign writing jobs based on what particular clients are asking for?

Melanie: All positions for Webwriters at the moment are with our E-cubation™ projects, so a Webwriter can pitch a particular project's development team. It's obviously best to understand the medium. We welcome all ideas, but we recommend you understand how your ideas will affect a specific project.

Q: How much technical expertise should a Webwriter have — raw HTML coding, experience with a particular WYSIWYG Web authoring tool, graphics applications, multimedia, cross-platform, etc.?

Melanie: The more a Webwriter knows about writing for the Internet, the better. We like our writers to know a bit of HTML, and at least know the different types of software we use. The ability to learn new things quickly is the key.

Q: Stratford Internet has expanded very rapidly in the past year. Based on that experience, what kinds of career opportunities (and hazards) do you foresee for Webwriters in the next year or two?

Melanie: As Stratford grows and the in-house projects it develops expand, there will be more opportunities for Webwriters. Understanding and staying on top of the process are key. The Internet has opened up a new medium for writers to get their work out to more people at a much faster pace.

Keeping on top of trends and keeping up with the demand, while consistently maintaining a high level of quality, may be a challenge. But the opportunities are infinite.

Can I teach Webwriting?

You can't do it all yourself. Someone in your company or school has to be able to write Web content besides you. So if you're the most experienced Webwriter around, chances are you'll end up teaching your colleagues or students how to write for the Web.

You can teach Webwriting successfully — especially if you set up your course or workshop so that your students really teach themselves. The principles that make a good Website are also the principles that make a good course.

Start with the key question: Who's your audience? How narrowly can you define it? Do you want to reach nuclear physicists, cancer patients, hiphop fans?

And who, therefore, are your students? Are they colleagues in your company, or students just passing through your classroom? Why do they want to learn Webwriting — to make themselves more employable in future, or to hang on to a job right now? Can they choose the kind of Website they're creating, or must they accept an existing site as their workspace?

The answers to those questions will help determine both your course content and the style and tone in which you express it. You'll have to take your students' strengths and weaknesses as your starting point.

Any good Website does the same thing: its purpose is to serve the user, not to flatter the creator. If your students don't know technical terms, then you'll have to avoid them (or define them clearly when you must use them). If they know XML but can't spell "extensible," then you'll have to spend time on correct spelling.

Coming out of a print-oriented business or school culture, your students will want to write long — but you know hypertext often works best in short, stand-alone chunks of 100 words or less. Students know when they're dealing with a good or bad site, but they may have trouble explaining why. And they may forget that this is an *interactive* medium that succeeds only when the user responds to the information on the site.

Here are six techniques to help your students teach themselves Webwriting:

1. Tell your students to write a 500-word essay. After you've returned it with your comments and corrections, announce their second assignment: To cut the first essay by 50 percent or more... and still have it hang together and make sense.

   Students are used to padding their essays with BS, but now the prize will go to the leanest, cleanest prose they can bring out of the first essay. You'll be amazed at how quickly and brutally they can cut their own work, and yours. (By the way, the first draft of this section was 1100 words long; it's now 789 words.)

2. Ask them to cut again until they get below that 100-word maximum for a chunk. They can't? Can they break the text into two chunks?

3. Further editing assignments, especially adapting long print text to the Web, will hone their skills and train them to find natural breaks between passages that can stand alone on the Web if need be.

4. Ask your students to write Website reviews. Let them use their own standards, or apply those of some usability wizard like Jakob Nielsen. By writing about those sites, your students will have to articulate their opinions, not just say: "This sucks, that doesn't."

5. Ask for detailed proposals for their own sites: purpose, intended audience, content... even the hours they estimate it will take them to write their Web content. Then they can rough out a site map or outline, without having to improvise or hope for sudden inspiration.

6. Put students' draft Webtext up on a chalkboard or overhead transparency so everyone can see it — and rip it apart. Is it short? Usable? Understandable? Does it invite response?

No doubt you'll want to do much more, but these assignments and activities have been the core of my own Webwriting course, and they've worked.

What's more, they've worked in a regular classroom, not in a computer lab. Put students in front of networked computers, and they're all over the planet before you can give them the first URL you want them to find. Use a single computer and a projector in a darkened classroom, and they fall asleep. If they're spending the rest of their day staring at a monitor, they'll be grateful not to have to do so in your class.

Plan on something else important: Your students won't just teach themselves. They'll teach *you* a lot about this medium and the way words work in it. The interactivity isn't just on the site — it'll happen in your class as well. And you'll go on learning something new every time you teach how to write for the Web.

Can I create my own e-zine?

Sure. The question is whether your e-zine will attract enough readers to interest advertisers. If it does, advertising will help pay the costs of the e-zine and maybe even pay you something. If it doesn't, your e-zine will be just a hobby.

As with any other form of self-publishing, you should consider whether you're a writer, a businessperson, or both. If you're primarily a writer, looking after the business end of running an e-zine will be time taken away from what you really enjoy doing. If you enjoy both writing and business, an e-zine could be an ideal way to combine your interests.

Can I be a journalist on the Web?

Yes, and many journalists are extremely busy on the Web. In some cases they're adapting print text to Webtext; in others, they're writing directly for the electronic medium. Print media, meanwhile, are turning to Web journalism as a source. Web reporter Matt Drudge broke important elements of the 1998-1999 President Clinton-Monica Lewinski scandal. Articles that first appeared in online journals like *Salon* are turning up in newspapers.

Significantly, online journals pay much more attention to Orientation than do newspapers and magazines. The table of contents in your morning paper is small and probably hard to find until you know where to look. The front page of *CNN Online*, by contrast, devotes as much space to links and navigation aids as to headline stories. Most online journals are still trying to choose between hit and run and archival structure for their news stories. Typically, a story will display a headline and an introductory paragraph that summarizes the story. Readers scroll down a series of these stories, hitting and running until they find something they want to learn more about; then they click on <u>Full Story</u> and find themselves scanning a multi-paragraph column of text essentially identical to the story as it might appear on paper.

Some online journals do exploit the Information aspect of the Web by supplying much more material than their print equivalents do. A current story may provide links to other recent articles on the same subject, enabling readers to place the current story in context.

When it comes to the Action aspect of Webwriting, however, online journalism still has a structural problem: What exactly is this highly informed public supposed to do in response to what it's learned? In traditional print media, action consists of writing letters to the editor, or phoning politicians to give them an earful; action may even consist of going to court. Online, however, action usually means clicking on still more stories providing still more information. Web journals may sometimes include email addresses of politicians or officials, inviting readers to bombard them with easy-to-send messages.

More often than their print counterparts, online journals ask readers for trivial or irrelevant responses. On the day in October 1998 that Microsoft went to court to defend itself against monopoly charges, *CNN Online* followed its story with an opinion poll, asking readers whether they thought Microsoft was indeed guilty of monopolistic practices. Since that was precisely what the US government and Microsoft were trying to determine in the trial, CNN's poll was nothing but a profile of ignorance; readers might act in response to what they'd read, but only on the level of a lynch mob.

The best way to learn online journalism is to read a lot of it and to read commentary on it. Here are the URLs of some very capable Web journals, journalists, and media commentators:

- Steve Outing ("Stop the Presses" columnist for the online version of *Editor & Publisher*): <http://www.mediainfo.com/ephome/news/newshtm/stop/stop.htm>

- Amy Gahran's *Contentious* (e-zine about content development issues): <http://www.contentious.com/>

- *Online Journalism Review* (e-zine survey of the subject; from University of Southern California): <http://ojr.usc.edu/>

- *Salon* (one of the most influential e-zines on the Web): <http://www.salon.com/>

- *Feed* (another good e-zine): <http://www.feedmag.com/>

- *The Atlantic Unbound* (online version of the influential monthly): <http://www.theatlantic.com/>

- *South China Morning Post* (a good online newspaper): <http://www.scmp.com/News/Front/>

- *Mercury Center* (online version of the *San Jose Mercury,* Silicon Valley's newspaper): <http://www.sjmercury.com>

- *January* (online book reviews): <http://www.januarymagazine.com/>

- *The Guardian Online* (British online newspaper; focus on computers): <http://www.guardian.co.uk/>

Can I write hypertext fiction for the Web?

Yes, but it's a highly demanding form in which no one has more than a few years' experience. If you are interested in exploring this genre, the best place to start is probably the Eastgate Systems home page:

<http://www.eastgate.com>

Eastgate has been actively promoting hypertext fiction since the late 1980s, and has published pioneering work in the field. Its site also supplies links to many other hypertext-fiction resources on the Web.

Other hypertext-fiction sites to visit are:

- *Hyperizons* (online magazine of hypertext fiction): <http://www.duke.edu/~mshumate/hyperfic.html>
- *101: onezeroone* (online magazine): <http://www.iceflow.com/onezeroone/101/OneZeroOne.html>

Can Webwriting be copyrighted?

Yes, but the issues surrounding intellectual property are complex and rapidly changing.

For example, some writers have found that when they sell an article to a print magazine, they've also unwittingly given away the electronic rights in perpetuity. The publishers can put the articles up on their magazines' Websites and use them to attract other readers, who in turn attract advertisers, who pay the publishers. But the publishers don't have to split that income with the writers, because the publishers hold the rights to the articles.

Many writers' organizations are fighting this practice, and freelancers are trying to get their publishers to state in advance exactly what rights they're buying. It will doubtless remain a vexing problem for years to come, especially in a medium where copying is so easy and copyright enforcement so difficult.

Meanwhile, you may find yourself violating someone else's copyright — knowingly or otherwise — by pasting parts of some Web-published document into your own work. It's always a good idea to get permission from

Copyright

Copyright law deals with intellectual property. In Canada and the United States, and in other countries that are members of the Berne Convention, writers of original work are automatically copyright holders of that work until they waive that exclusive right, or in special circumstances, such as work-for-hire.

Note that it is the words used to express an idea that are copyrighted; the ideas themselves are not.

the copyright holder before you use even a graphic from someone else's site. You may find that the holder of the copyright will grant permission to copy in return for a link on your site to the original item.

The following Websites should give you a general sense of how copyright affects you and your work:

- Electronic Frontier Foundation (an important site for many other resources as well):
  <http://www.eff.org/pub/Intellectual_property/>

- Intellectual Property on the Net:
  <http://www.cpsr.org/program/nii/IP.html>

- Digital Future Coalition: <http://www.dfc.org>

- International Federation of Library Associations: Copyright and Intellectual Property: <http://www.ifla.org/II/cpyright.htm>

- World Intellectual Property Organization:
  <http://www.wipo.int/>

- US Copyright Office: <http://lcweb.loc.gov/copyright/>

- American Society of Journalists and Authors: The Basics About Copyright Registration: <http://www.asja.org/>

How do I cite Web sources in scholarly writing?

The Web is becoming an indispensable research tool (and, alas, a resource for plagiarists), but it's happened so fast that authorities are still developing standard forms of citation. Generally accepted types of citations follow this basic format:

Author. "Article Title." <u>Periodical/Book Title</u>. Date given on Web page. Date accessed by reader. Length in paragraphs. <URL>.

The author's name appears last name first (if the item has more than one author, subsequent authors appear with first name first). The title of the article appears in quotation marks, with a period inside the close quotation. The name of the period or book appears with the main words capitalized and the whole title underlined. The date of the Web page is given as well as the date you accessed it, since of course the page may well have changed since you did so. Paragraph length is a substitute for page length, and it may be tedious to count paragraphs. However, your readers will at least know if the source is a long one. The URL appears with <> around it to set it off from nearby letters and punctuation marks that some readers might think are part of the URL.

To give some examples:

Journal Articles:

Author. "Article Title." Journal Title. Volume. Issue (Year): paging or length in paragraphs (pars). Access date (date you obtained the file). Uniform Resource Locator (URL) — the Web address.

Flannagan, Roy. "Reflections on Milton and Ariosto." Early Modern Literary Studies 2.3 (1996): 16 pars. 22 Feb. 1997. <http://unixg.ubc.ca:7001/0/e-sources/emls/02-3/flanmilt.html>

Magazine Articles:

Author. "Article Title." Magazine Title. Date: paging or length in paragraphs. Access date. <URL>.

Achenbach, Joel. "What Do You Say to a Naked Alien?" *Slate*. 22 November 1999. 19 pars. 23 November 1999. <http://slate/msn.com/Features/Achenbach/Achenbach.asp>

Books on the Web:

Author(s). Book Title. Date. Publisher or sponsoring organization. Access date. <URL>.

Kilian, Crawford, Leslie Savage, Azza Sedky & Martin Wittman. The Communications Book: Writing for the Workplace. September 1998. Capilano College. 7 February 2000. <http://www.capcollege.bc.ca/magic/cmns/textbook.html>

Newspaper Articles:

Author. "Article Title." Newspaper title. Date, Edition (if given): paging or length in paragraphs. Access date. <URL>.

Adams, Michael and Amy Langstaff. "You Say Paternal .. And I Say Relax." *The Globe & Mail*. July 3, 2000: 22 pars. July 7, 2000.

<http://www.globeandmail.ca/gam/Commentary/20000703/COAD-AMY.html>

Personal Site:

Author. Home page. Access date. <URL>.

Kilian, Crawford. Home page. 20 January 2000. <http://www.capcollege.bc.ca/magic/cmns/crofpers.html>

Corporate Site:

Organization name. "Page Title." Date (if given): paging or length in paragraphs. Access date. <URL>.

Canadian Alliance Against Software Theft. "Stats at a Glance." 21 Feb. 1999: 5 pars. 18 March 1999. <http://www.caast.org/theft/stats/stats.asp>

For more detailed guidelines, consult these online resources:

- Citation Styles Online
  <http://www.bedsfordstmartins.com/online/citex/html
- Columbia Guide to Online Style
  <http://www.columbia.edu/cu/cup/cgos/idx_basic.html>
- Electronic Citation Style Guides (University of Texas at El Paso Library)
  <http://libraryweb.utep.edu/ref/citing.html>
- Meta-Index to Citation Guides
  <http://bailiwick.lib.uiowa.edu/journalism/cite.html>

Can a book on paper be enhanced with a Website?

Yes. More and more textbooks offer Websites as a way to update and expand their print content. Other kinds of books will no doubt do the same. In nonfiction, Websites will enable content to stay current without producing a whole new print edition.

In fiction (and nonfiction as well, no doubt), Websites will give readers an opportunity to respond directly to the author and publisher. This is already happening even when authors and publishers don't yet have their own sites: On the Amazon.com bookselling site, for example, visitors can post their own reviews of books they've read, and authors can respond — authors can even review their own books if they like!

Many publishers are already posting excerpts from print books on the Web as a way to stir up interest in the book. This follows a practice of some paperback publishing houses, which may include an excerpt from a forthcoming book in the back of another novel — like the Coming Attractions at a movie. Some publishers are even putting whole manuscripts online. Readers can either read the whole book on-screen (often paying to do so), or pay for a custom-printed copy. Authors themselves are divided on the value of such schemes.

Can I write courses to be taken over the Web?

Online education has grown explosively in the past decade. According to the Higher Education Research Institute at UCLA, American colleges and universities have more than doubled their online courses and programs since 1994. Fully half of the 5,000 post-secondaries in the US now offer some kind of distance education, and over 60 percent of those courses use Internet technology. Many also use "distributed learning," which means a mix of print, Internet media, and material on CD-ROMs.

Unfortunately, much online-learning content is "shovelware," material designed for print on paper and simply uploaded onto course Websites. That may be all right if the students can then download and print out the material — but in that case, why not just mail them the textbook and handouts in the first place?

Another hazard: Students in many online courses tend to drop out, or to do less well than they would have in a face-to-face course. A major reason is that text designed for print is harder to read and respond to on the computer monitor.

British Columbia's Open Learning Agency (OLA) is keenly aware of these problems, and its expertise is in strong demand — not only in Canada, but in countries like Mexico and India, where OLA is designing whole distance-education systems.

Recently I spoke with David Porter, executive director of learning systems at OLA, about what it takes to write courses for the online medium. For many online writers, he told me, the career path may be as "subject matter expert" (SME) or as a media-smart editor.

"We use a team approach," Porter told me, "that consists of an instructional designer, instructional media producer, graphic artist, instructor/ tutor, and various editors (copy and substantive). In most cases we hire a subject matter expert to write the materials, but our assumption is that this person does not necessarily have a deep, formal background in… the appropriate use of instructional media."

A subject-matter expert needs "knowledge at a high level that is current and relevant," says Porter. "Experience with distance and distributed learning is another criterion, as is the ability to work in a team environment and take direction from a project manager who sets design and writing tasks. For academic disciplines SMEs might be professors or technically trained professionals with Master's degrees or PhDs."

A writer might create brand-new material (for niche courses) or "wrap" available resources (Websites, texts, videos, etc.) for more generic courses like introductory English or psychology. The subject-matter expert works with the instructional designer, who, says Porter, functions as a managing editor.

Does it help to get formal training? "Instructional design and course authoring techniques would be a good background to have," says Porter.

Simply knowing different software applications may not be enough. "Most software that includes a developmental environment for authoring online has an implied instructional design embedded. Unfortunately, in many cases this results in the automation of lecture notes and produces a kind of shovelware that may or may not be effective."

Apart from writing skill, what does a coursewriter need? "The biggest assets," Porter says, "would be current, relevant knowledge of the subject area and its creative presentation, the ability to function as a team member, and the ability to write to specification. In this sense it would be more like magazine writing than writing a novel. Unfortunately, I have seen projects killed off at the first draft stage because the SME, while knowledgeable, was way off the mark from an instructional perspective."

Keeping the learner in mind is critical. "The biggest job I have with my instructional designers," says Porter, "is to help them understand their role as project managers, to explicitly describe the course from a learner/customer perspective in the planning document (business plan) and to clearly map the expectations (via contract) with the course writer for writing content, selecting resources, creating activities, and matching assessment strategies with course outcomes — the logical links between the beginning and end of a course."

For online corporate training, emphasis is on measurable results — improved performance and demonstrated skill mastery. What's more, says Porter, the results must advance organizational goals or the financial bottom line. "Most companies spend big money on training and expect measurable performance as an outcome. So training programs tend to build performance measures into courses that can be validated explicitly in a workplace context."

Payment for OLA's online writers is strictly fee for service, says Porter. "This can vary based upon their knowledge, experience, online cachet, and their demonstrated ability to work to specification in the team environment." Relatively inexperienced SMEs may learn through a series of small contracts, he says. Regardless of experience, fees are negotiated case by case. "It has a lot to do with whether there will be a lot of original writing, or whether the course will simply be a 'wrap.' In all cases, we purchase all rights. There is no royalty relationship."

You can't really specialize in one medium, says Porter. "We expect our writers to think about print and electronic presentations of the content in all projects. The reality is that learners are the driver and they come in many flavors and from multiple situations. We expect to produce our courses in multiple media — print, online, and CD — and for each the expectations for presentation are slightly different."

And the career prospects? "The demand for effective course writers in the electronic space is going to go way up over the next five years," says Porter.

AFTERWORD

In a book about interactive writing, no one has the last word — least of all the author. Whether you've read this book in linear fashion, or hopped around as if it were hypertext, you've been engaged in some kind of dialogue with it. Maybe you scribbled in the margins, or threw the book across the room. Maybe you changed your personal Website, or left it exactly as it was just to show how unimpressive you found my arguments.

But the Web is designed for dialogue as print is not. If you have questions, comments, objections, or worries about what you've read here, by all means let me know. You can reach me at:

- <ckilian@thehub.capcollege.bc.ca>

and you can see my own Websites at:

- <http://www.capcollege.bc.ca/magic/cmns/crofpers.html> (personal site) and
- <http://www.capcollege.bc.ca/magic/cmns/fwp.html> (Fiction Writer's Page).

I look forward to hearing from you — even by snail mail!

Crawford Kilian
Communications Department
Capilano College
2055 Purcell Way
North Vancouver, BC V7J 3H5

APPENDIX 1: EXERCISE KEY

Exercise 1: Converting Prose to Bullets

The key conventions of modern science fiction:

- Isolated society (island, lost valley, planet)
- Morally significant language (Orwell's Newspeak)
- Important documents (Book of Bokonon in Vonnegut's *Cat's Cradle*)
- Ideological attitude toward sex (Huxley's *Brave New World*)
- An inquisitive outsider (Genly Ai in Le Guin's *The Left Hand of Darkness*)

  [48 words]

Exercise 2: Activating the Passive

Here are active-voice versions of the passive-voice sentences. Other versions could be equally acceptable.

1. Some researchers argue that the US Air Force retrieved alien bodies from a crashed spacecraft near Roswell, New Mexico, in 1947.

2. Critics hailed Miles Davis's "Sketches of Spain" as one of his finest works.

3. Researchers at Xerox originally developed the graphic user interface.

4. A local physician stopped a 19th-century outbreak of cholera in London by removing the handle from a neighborhood water pump.

5. We carefully chose these graphics to illustrate each step of the process.

Exercise 3: Using Anglo-Saxon Vocabulary

1. Altercation: angry dispute

2. Antagonist: adversary, opponent

3. Capitulate: give up, surrender

4. Celestial: pertaining to the sky or heavens

5. Demotic: common, popular

6. Epitome: typical (or extreme) example; concise summary

7. Fiduciary: acting as trustee or guardian; held in trust

8. Gravamen: most serious part of an accusation; essential part or gist

9. Impediment: obstacle, handicap

10. Litigious: quarrelsome, quick to go to court

Exercise 4: Editing for Clear, Short Webtext

I suggested you cut this 277-word passage down to 100 words maximum (the length of a chunk). If that seemed impossible, you could try to break it into no more than two chunks, each with its own title. A single 100-word chunk probably wouldn't convey much, but consider the following two chunks:

Chesterton's Early History

Built in 1891 by the Chesterton Logging Company, the town soon grew to over 3,000. During World War I, Chesterton grew to 4,000 to provide spruce to build airplanes. A postwar zinc mine at the base of Mount Freeman brought prosperity in the late 1920s, even after the original sawmill shut down. But in the Great Depression the zinc market collapsed and hundreds of workers lost their jobs. Chesterton's population shrank to not much more than 300. *[77 words]*

Chesterton's Recent History

After World War II, the creation of Chesterton Regional Park revived the town. As tourism grew, the community began catering to skiers, hikers, and campers. Chesterton now offers world-class skiing at High Corniche, the North American Kayak Championships at Roaring Creek, and a booming whitewater rafting business that puts almost 200 rafts into the Old Horse River every summer. With 12,000 year-round residents, Chesterton is now a major recreation center and eco-tourism destination. <u>Details on accommodations and recreation facilities</u>. *[79 words]*

Exercise 5: Editing a News Release

Edited and shortened news release

Chesterton's first Folk Music Festival will take place at Green River Park on July 5, 6, and 7. The opening-night concert will feature Cajun singer-songwriter Marc Belliveau, whose latest CD has just been released. Other singers and groups will include Carolyn Loewen, Dora Hardy, and the Mexican women's quartet Las Golondrinas. The Green River Gang, Chesterton's local folk trio, will also perform. Many local ethnic restaurants will serve food at booths in the park. The Chesterton Folk Music Society estimates that 20,000 people will attend at least part of the festival. "We're really excited about the event," says society president Mary O'Reilley. "For three days, Chesterton will be the center of the folk world." Tickets will be $50 for all three days, or $25/day. *[124 words]*

What's New

Our first Folk Music Festival will make Green River Park the center of the folk world from July 5 to 7! Enjoy live performances from Marc Belliveau, Carolyn Loewen, Dora Hardy, Las Golondrinas, and our own Green River Gang. Tickets: $25/day or $50 for all three days. *[47 words]*

APPENDIX 2: HYPERTEXT STYLE

For several years, Web design pioneer Gareth Rees maintained a very helpful Hypertext Style Guide Web page. He recently removed it, but has kindly given me permission to reproduce it here, slightly abridged.

This material is intended to supplement the CERN Style Guide <http://www.w3.org/pub/WWW/Provider/Style/Overview.html>, not to replace it. Some of it is appropriate to people with big data bases of material to organize; other bits are directed at people with lame home pages.

Present Coherent Articles as a Whole

Readers understand coherent articles — they see them all the time in magazines, newspapers, journals, and conference proceedings. They don't have much experience of reading articles that have been chopped into pieces — and just as importantly, neither do you. If you choose to present your information in a form close to existing forms, then you know what is successful in that form and what isn't. If you choose to adopt a new form, then you had better think very carefully about exactly how to structure your text for best effect. Read the literature on hypertext for a discussion of how to structure documents for readability; test your documents on readers as though they were computer programs with strange new user interfaces (which, in a sense, they are).

In most browsers, it's easier to navigate within a page than between pages. Dividing a single text into a number of pages, or chunks, means your readers will have to issue a lot of navigational commands to read it.

If you chop your material into small chunks, then readers are prevented from following the thread of your argument because of the long wait for each paragraph to download. If your material is presented as one long, scrolling page, then the initial wait is longer, but once the article has been downloaded the reader can give it his or her full attention.

If you have space, the best solution may be to take advantage of the medium of hypertext and present your article in both ways (as a single complete article and as a multiplicity of paragraphs) and let the reader choose, depending on his or her preference.

Make Sure Deep Structure Is Accessible

In a deep hypertext structure, with indexes at several levels, it is possible for information to be "lost" in the sense that a reader reading the top-level index will be unaware of the existence of deeper information.

This is most likely to happen if different levels of indexes organize information according to different criteria. For example, suppose that a hypothetical university information server has a home page that indexes the home pages of the departments in that university, but doesn't say what information those departments provide. In such a case, the reader must guess which department has the information you need before you can find it.

It is therefore important to provide clues at each level indicating what is to be found on each of the branches. Hierarchical subject trees are examples where this works, because the choices at each level provide access to subsets of the subjects named at the level above. Having a clear index structure also helps you to give an impression of the size of your data base.

A good way to prevent your readers getting "lost in hyperspace" (a common feeling when browsing a complex structure) is to give them plenty of clues as to how big your data base is.

The best clue you can provide is a complete listing of entries (even if such a list isn't appropriate on the home page, it can be provided separately). A top-level index of categories should annotate each entry with the number of documents to be found by following that entry. If you can find an appropriate visual organizing principle, then a graphical overview might help those of your readers with fast connections and graphical browsers. To give a correct impression of the size of your data base, you need to distinguish internal and external links.

Some home pages freely mix links pointing to documents in the data base at that site with documents stored elsewhere, as though the Web were a single amorphous information resource. But amorphous doesn't necessarily imply useful.

If you maintain a personal home page, then —

(a) *Never use your home page as the startup page for your browser.* The startup page for a browser is a place where you put all the links you use regularly, especially including the major libraries and meta-indexes on the Web. On the other hand, your home page is a document that describes you to the rest of the world and lists the resources that can be found in your data base. So why confuse the two?

(b) *Don't use links as footnotes.* Footnotes distract from a line of argument; if the material in a footnote can't be integrated into the body of the text, it probably doesn't belong in a footnote either. Just because you can include jottings, notes, side issues, and other material in a hypertext document, doesn't mean you have to.

(c) *Annotate your references.* Please, annotate your lists. Try to provide a short description of the contents of the destination of the link (but use your discretion; some titles are self-explanatory, and a blurb that says nothing useful is as bad as no blurb at all). Think of it as your way of adding value to the list; anyone can compile a list of links (the Web-crawling robots have data bases with hundreds of thousands of URLs), but you have to read and understand the documents in order to write useful descriptions and thus make your list a valuable resource.

(d) *Don't discuss your own pages.* The mere lack of anything to say doesn't stop some people; instead of writing about the world "out there," they discuss their own Web pages — how they were written, when they were written, what's new about them, what their friends had to say about them, what the usage statistics are, who's read them, and so on.

GLOSSARY

This book uses many terms that have become standard in Webwriting, but they're often baffling to "newbies" — newcomers to the world of the Internet. Here are brief definitions of some of the terms people have the most trouble with:

archive (verb): to store a document on a Website, usually the full text of something originally written for print on paper; the document is not likely to be changed or updated.

blurb (noun): a short description of what readers can expect if they follow a particular link.

browser (noun): a software program that can find and display the files of a Website (e.g., Netscape or Internet Explorer). In effect, the browser copies the files temporarily onto your computer. It will also let you download a permanent copy of the text, graphics, and other elements.

chunk (verb or noun): create short passages of text that can be displayed on a single screen. Chunking can include either breaking up longer text into independent segments, or writing brief passages from scratch. A chunk of text is usually no more than 100 words long, and may be much shorter.

cookie (noun): a piece of information that a Website can install on your computer. When you return to that site, it will recognize you from your cookie and may display the site as you requested on your last visit.

download (verb): copy a file from another Website. This may be a text file, a graphic, or a whole software application.

email (noun or verb): electronic mail — messages sent over the Internet. Such messages may include copies of earlier messages. Many Websites include email addresses enabling readers to send messages to the site's creator or persons connected to it in some way. As a verb: "I'll email the changes to you this afternoon."

e-zine (noun): a Website in the form of an electronic magazine, including articles, pictures, sound, and other effects. An e-zine may be the creation of a single person, or of many contributors. Some are paying markets for freelance writers.

FAQs (noun): frequently asked questions. Pronounced "facks." A list of questions and answers on a given topic, often included on a Website to save its creator from tediously repeating the same answers.

flame (verb): send insulting and abusive messages by email, often in response to a real or perceived insult or abuse — for example, posting the same message in many different newsgroups, or criticizing someone for his or her spelling or grammar.

frame (noun): component of a Web page that has been divided so that some parts always remain visible; convenient for navigating large sites with many links, but frames also reduce the amount of space available for a particular text or graphic.

front page (noun): the introductory page of a Website, often containing introductory comments and a table of contents.

hit and run (adjective): used to describe both a method of information retrieval — scanning and moving on to another item — and the kind of item most easily scanned; this is usually a single chunk of text, visible on a single screen without the need to scroll down it.

home page (noun): synonynm for "front page," but also used to mean a whole Website with more information on its topic than any other such site; your personal page is your "home page," for example, but your page celebrating Holly Cole may not be *her* home page.

hook (noun): an unusual statement (or graphic) that draws and holds attention so that users will read an entire file or explore a major part of a site.

HTML (noun): hypertext markup language. A simple code that turns text and graphics into something that a Web browser can display.

hypertext (noun): an electronic file containing a document (or part of a document) with electronic links to other documents. A hypertext may exist on a CD-ROM, such as an encyclopedia, as a "help" file in a software application, or on a Website. A single graphic, if it contains links to other graphics or text files, is also hypertext. The term "hypertext" applies both to an individual file with its links, and to all the other files it links to.

Internet (noun): the network of networks permitting access to computers (and their contents) around the world.

jolt (noun): a sensory or intellectual stimulus created or transmitted by computer — for example, a sound file that announces, "You've got mail," or an animated image, or an emotionally charged email message.

keyword (noun): a word or phrase used to help identify a file that may be of interest. "Spaghetti alla primavera" could be a keyword in a search for Italian recipes; "Web style" could be a keyword in a search for advice on writing Webtext.

link (noun or verb): a word, phrase, or graphic on a Web page, containing the address of another electronic file. Clicking the cursor on a link commands the browser to seek that address and to display its content. Also, to create or provide such an address: "This page also links to other sites offering advice on Italian cooking."

listserv (noun): an electronic discussion group focused on a particular topic. Everyone belonging to the listserv receives messages posted from other members to the listserv, and can send messages to all other members. Members must subscribe to listservs, unlike newsgroups, which are open to anyone with a "newsreader" software application.

meta-tag (noun): an invisible word or phrase that provides a keyword, located at the top of a Web page. Search engines sometimes list pages by the number of times they find the keyword; a site with an invisible meta-tag that says "primavera primavera primavera primavera" will turn up sooner than a site that just says "Spaghetti alla primavera." Some search engines, however, are programmed to reject such meta-tags. The purpose of the meta-tag is to attract more visits by readers (or "hits") so the Website can charge more to advertisers.

navigation bar (noun): a part of the Website, usually visible on every page, that permits movement among various pages as well as movement to pages on other sites.

navigation button (noun): an image that provides a link to another part of a site — for example, to the home page or the index page.

online (adjective or adverb): referring to the Internet or World Wide Web. "She reviewed several online résumés" (résumés stored in a computer linked to the Web). "He researched online for several hours" (went from one Website to another looking for information). Can also refer to materials that are stored on CD-ROM or as part of a software application, as in Online Help.

pdf (noun): portable document format. A way of storing and displaying files so that, using the Adobe Acrobat reader (a free software application), the files appear with all their original formatting, fonts, graphics, and other details.

plug-in (noun): a software extension that "plugs in" to your browser so you see or hear some special aspect of a Website. RealAudio, for example, lets you hear an audio file while it is downloading.

resolution (noun): the fineness of detail available on a computer screen; a high-resolution screen provides a sharper, clearer image than a low-resolution screen.

scrolling (verb or adjective): moving a long text file up or down the computer screen. Many readers dislike scrolling; some long, scrolling texts contain internal links that enable readers to go straight to the section of interest.

search engine (noun): a program that rapidly searches millions of Web and Internet files for the keyword you have specified. The engine will then display what it has found, with the likeliest pages first. Meta-search engines enlist the help of many other search engines and therefore search a wider range of files. For example, if you use Dogpile to find "spaghetti alla primavera," that meta-search engine will ask AltaVista, Yahoo!, and many other search engines to take part in the search.

shareware (noun): a software application that you can download from the Web without payment. The application may erase itself after a trial period, or display an annoying message until you have paid for it and received a code that will disable the message. Some shareware programs aren't fully functional until paid for.

splash page (noun): an introductory page, often a dramatic graphic, used on some sites; the user must click on it to reach the real front page of the Website.

stack (verb or noun): connect two or more chunks of Web text with a link. If your recipe for spaghetti alla primavera is a chunk, and you provide a link to a recipe for spaghetti trastevere, you have created a stack.

stickiness (noun): the quality of content and display in a Website that encourages users to "stick around" to explore it.

surf (verb): to move from one Website to another, especially on impulse.

template (noun): a preformatted Web page, into which the Website creator can insert text and graphics; often used where a consistent look and feel is desired on a large site, or where the Website creator doesn't want to manually repeat the same basic design steps.

upload (verb): to send a computer file to another computer elsewhere on the Internet.

URL (noun): uniform resource locator. The address of a Website. It tells your browser where to look for a particular page. In many cases, the browser will assume it's a commercial site if you simply type in the company name. If you ask your browser to Open File and then type in "microsoft," it will automatically seek out <http://www.microsoft.com> and open the Microsoft Corporation's home page.

Web authoring software (noun): a program that makes it easier to create the HTML you need to build and display a Web page. Some Web authoring programs are simple shareware. Others are sophisticated and expensive.

Webmaster (noun): the person responsible for maintaining a Website. The Webmaster may also create the site or may allow others to create and upload pages to the site.

Web page (noun): a single file displaying text, graphics, or sound, usually linked to one or more pages.

Website (noun): a number of Web pages linked to one another and usually dealing with closely related topics; a Website is usually located on a single "server" (networked computer).

World Wide Web (noun): the entire system of sites and their content files accessible by browser from anywhere in the world.

Permissions

The author wishes to acknowledge that the following have generously given permission to reproduce their materials, in whole or in part, in this book:

In Case Study 1, the essay "Designing for an Audience of One" by John S. Rhodes and Bill Skeet.

In Chapter 6, a quotation from personal correspondence with Stephen Martin.

In Case Study 3, the Website Freelancin' Babes International by Karen Solomon.

In Case Study 4, the essay "Why Won't Some Managers Clean Up Their Act?" by Lisa Schmitt.

In Case Study 5, the Website Aunt Jessie's Bed and Breakfast by Alex and Irene Kirkwood.

In Chapter 9, the list of Websites provided by Tara Calishain.

OTHER TITLES IN THE
SELF-COUNSEL BUSINESS SERIES

GETTING PUBLICITY
Tana Fletcher and Julia Rockler
$20.95

- Put together a publicity plan
- Create publicity opportunities
- Understand the media
- Master the media interview

If you'd like to know all the inside secrets for attracting publicity to your business, your association, or yourself, you need this book. Step-by-step instructions illustrate just what it takes for any enterprise to generate media attention.

The authors, both award-winning journalists, show how you can make the most of every opportunity for free coverage in print, broadcast, and Internet media.

From newspaper articles to radio interviews, from television appearances to the World Wide Web, this expanded and updated edition includes all the advice you need to sparkle in the publicity spotlight.

WRITING FREELANCE
Christine Adamec
$19.95

- Turn talent into dollars
- Understand the business of writing
- Communicate with editors and clients
- Find out if you have what it takes

Do you want to be a writer and make money? Are you someone with interesting ideas and an intense curiosity about a subject or many different subjects? Have you pushed this side of yourself into the shadows because you equated writing with poverty?

Writing Freelance will show you how to succeed in turning your talent and skill into dollars. This book not only covers the advantages and disadvantages of being a freelance writer, but also the nuts-and-bolts issues of running a successful business. It delves into who hires writers and why, what the essential traits of a freelance writer are, and how to plan and set goals.

CYBERLAW CANADA
Jeffrey M. Schelling, LLB
$16.95

Businesses are now more than ever before taking advantage of the speed and ease of electronic communication and the opportunity for sales over the Internet. But the laws regulating the Internet will have a significant impact on our daily lives and on our businesses. *Cyberlaw Canada* equips you to deal with straightforward legal matters and recognize when you need legal advice.

Everyone who uses a computer needs to be aware of the legal principles applying to Internet use (and misuse). As the many applications of the Web increase, so do the risks involved. This complete guide goes beyond merely explaining the law, offering practical advice for preventing legal infringements.

Includes advice on:

- Liability and negligence
- Secure on-line commercial transactions
- Electronic contracts
- Copyright and the Internet
- Privacy of electronic information
- Domain-name disputes

ORDER FORM

All prices are subject to change without notice. Books are available in book, department, and stationery stores. If you cannot buy the book through a store, please use this order form. (Please print.)

Name _____

Address _____

Charge to: ❏ Visa ❏ MasterCard

Account Number _____

Validation Date _____

Expiry Date _____

Signature _____

Shipping and handling will apply.

In Canada, 7% GST will be added.

In Washington, 7.8% sales tax will be added.

Yes, please send me the following:

_____ *Getting Publicity*

_____ *Writing Freelance*

_____ *Cyberlaw Canada*

Please add $3.50 for postage and handling.

❏ Check here for a free catalogue.

IN THE USA
Self-Counsel Press, Inc.
1704 N. State Street
Bellingham, WA 98225

IN CANADA
Please send your order to the nearest location:

Self-Counsel Press
1481 Charlotte Road
North Vancouver, BC
V7J 1H1

Self-Counsel Press
4 Bram Court
Brampton, ON
L6W 3R6

Visit our Web site: *www.self-counsel.com*